THE
SAVOY
FOOD AND DRINK BOOK

Vincent Brooks Day & Son Lith.

"Royal English Opera."

RICHARD D'OYLY CARTE

THE
SAVOY
FOOD AND DRINK BOOK

To Raymon

Best Wishes !

PYRAMID

EDITOR: ALISON LEACH
PHOTOGRAPHY: PETER WILLIAMS
CONSULTANT ART DIRECTOR: RAYMOND HAWKEY
DESIGNERS: CHRISTOS KONDEATIS AND ROY TREVELION
COOKERY CONSULTANT: JANE SUTHERING

First published in Great Britain 1988 by
Pyramid an imprint of the Octopus Publishing Group
Michelin House 81 Fulham Road London SW3

Designed and produced by Genesis Productions Limited
30 Great Portland Street London W1N 5AD

ISBN 1-871307-14-7

Colour separations by Val Haven Limited, London
Printed and bound in Spain by Cayfosa Industria Gráfica S.A., Barcelona

CONTENTS

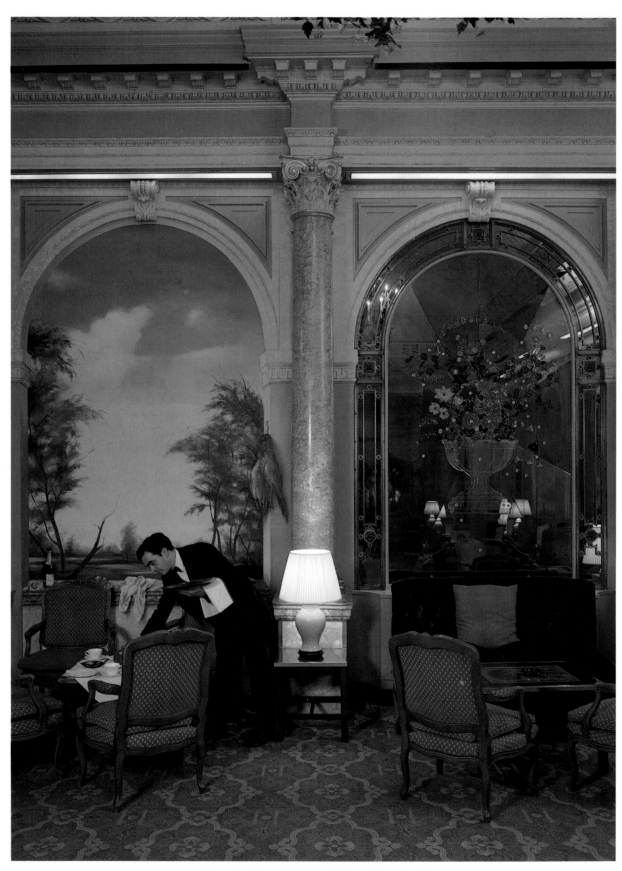

LINCOLN TABER'S TROMPE L'OEIL MURAL IN THE
THAMES FOYER

INTRODUCTION

The folk-lore I imbibed about The Savoy as a lad in the thirties said of course that it was grand and sumptuous, but in a quiet, reserved sort of way, not flashy or foreign or frequented by the mysterious adventuresses' I was reading about in the works of Sapper and Dornford Yates. When my father mentioned The Savoy, which admittedly was not all that often, it was always in tones of great respect. This may have been something to do with the fact that he was a terrific Gilbert and Sullivan fan, like all the family (except me). But anyway, The Savoy was one of those unique places that made London what it was and would always be there, like Big Ben, St Paul's, Lord's cricket ground and, not a mile off along the Embankment, my father's school and mine, the City of London.

In the long years when my idea of a large evening out was dinner for two at Morgan's Tudor Grill, Swansea, I had few chances to check my early impressions of The Savoy. But times changed, I became an author and was summoned in due course to be regaled by my publisher, the illustrious Victor Gollancz, at the Savoy Restaurant, where he was said to have lunch *every day*. This seemed to me an almost ridiculously high level on which to be living, one that brought some risk of becoming over-stuffed with luxuries, though it was a risk I personally might have considered taking at the time, given the chance. Of course I know better now.

Up I turned on the dot and was taken straight to the great man's regular table by the window – no time-wasting nonsense in bar or lounge before going in. Nor was any apéritif mentioned when I had settled myself. (It was not our first meeting.) Quite soon, in fact, Victor was studying the menu.

'I think tomato salad sounds the sort of thing to go for, don't you?' he said. 'It's always good here.'

'Oh, fine with me.'

'And then the chef does a very nice steak-and-kidney pie on Thursdays.'

'Does he now?'

I reasoned that today must be Thursday or Victor would probably not have bothered to mention that pie. I also reasoned that not only had I not yet been allowed a peep at a menu but that I was never going to see one if I sat there till tea-time. This ploy was new to me and I like to think I had the waiter's sympathy, but there was nothing to be done by either of us.

'And I don't know about you,' said my host, 'but I'm going to have some beer.'

Old Victor Gollancz was famous for his great way with the English language but even he never came up with anything more brilliant than that last remark. The steak-and-kidney pie turned out to be delicious, I remember, and the beer suited me down to the ground. Nevertheless I must have promised myself there and then that my future relations with The Savoy were not going to be on those lines.

Everything was as different as could be on the day in 1984 when I went down there to attend the lunch to celebrate Eric Ambler's 75th birthday. I had come straight from the memorial service in Westminster Abbey for an old friend, John Betjeman, and I needed good company and good cheer. They were there in plenty in the Patience Room. Ambler, the man who by universal consent invented the modern spy thriller, was being honoured by a gathering of thriller writers of more recent vintage: Anthony Price, Gavin Lyall, John le Carré, H. R. F. Keating, John Gardner, Frederick Forsyth, Julian Symons, Len Deighton, Lionel Davidson, Miles Tripp, Ted Allbeury. I sneaked in as the pseudonymous author of a one-off James Bond pastiche, and I felt I too was being honoured in a smaller way by being invited.

Far from immediately, we sat down to eat – we would have been thirteen at table but for The Savoy tradition of adding Kaspar to the company in such circumstances. Kaspar is a large doll in catlike form, rather horrifyingly appropriate, I thought, among chroniclers of dark and fearful deeds. He had little to say but everyone else had a lot. All of us made speeches, some of us in instalments. In one of mine I toasted everybody present, saying enthusiastically but truthfully that at different times each of them had added to my pleasure in life, also saying no less truthfully but more plaintively that I could think of no other assemblage in the world – certainly not a bunch of poets, for instance – where I could have said as much. More speeches and refreshment followed. Finally, in an operation as skilful as any in his novels, Len Deighton picked up the bill and made his getaway unseen.

It must have been later, not then, that I reviewed the occasion more objectively. The way the whole deal had been handled, the absence of the fuss-plus-muddle I had thought was inevitable at functions in private rooms, the feeling that you were completely secluded and yet could be brought anything you wanted in five seconds – well, it all showed me what was *possible*. And it was grand enough without either servility or condescension, something a boy from south of the river never forgets to appreciate.

A couple of years later, having come some distance from those early Gollancz days, I managed to win the Booker Prize for Fiction with my novel *The Old Devils*. Winning a thing like that, you know, is not like winning the 1000 metres at Wembley: it is no less exhausting but it takes much, much longer to happen. The first stage came when I was signing copies at a bookshop in Covent Garden and was urgently summoned to the telephone – I was on the short list! By what felt like an inevitable process, a law of nature, I found myself a few seconds afterwards, in the presence of a contingent from my publishers, drinking a large Dry Martini in the cocktail bar of The Savoy. This venue was already well known to me as a good place to entertain pretty young American graduate students. Later that evening and far from where I had started I was promised a lift home by a new acquaintance, a very merry fellow who kept saying we would be off just as soon as he had had another drink. No alternative seemed feasible. Growing alarm had begun to sober me up when he produced a Mercedes with a liveried chauffeur in it.

When the time came, and much to my permanent gratitude and satisfaction and the relief of those responsible for my finances, I finally and irreversibly won the Booker. My publishers had served me well enough, and been nice enough to me, for me to consider I owed them something. I further considered I owed myself something for the ceremonial dinner I had been unable to eat for all sorts of reasons, one of which was that it was uneatable. (Not that I would hold that against anybody faced with the task of serving up a full-dress meal for a couple of hundred in the vast, chilly Guildhall.) As before, what more natural and inevitable than a little private lunch at The Savoy? A handy rendezvous for my publishers from their offices in Chandos Place, sure, but that was not going to cut any ice with me, to whom anywhere in London or most of the Home Counties would have been handy that day, and whose treat was it? No, it *had* to be The Savoy.

Not many people will be surprised to learn that my memory of the occasion is not detailed. We assembled in the Iolanthe Room and from beginning to end the whole show went swimmingly. There was smoked salmon and a very good rack of lamb, there was a great deal of champagne and a certain amount of claret and not a little vintage port. And there was probably quite a lot of vaunting, vainglorious talk, led by me. Almost certainly I quoted an aphorism of that hoary old American novelist, Gore Vidal: 'It is not enough to succeed; others must fail,' – well, it was our day. I am quite positive we agreed that, when I get my dukedom or am appointed Archbishop of Canterbury, whichever comes first, we will reconvene, and in the self-same place.

After all, where else is there?

KINGSLEY AMIS

THE SAVOY HOTEL.

AN ENGRAVING FROM THE 'ILLUSTRATED LONDON NEWS' OF 1889

ONE HUNDRED GLORIOUS YEARS

Like all great institutions, The Savoy has a motto. In the early days, it was *Noscitur a sociis* – literally 'It is recognised among friends', perhaps better rendered as 'Birds of a feather flock together'. Since the Second World War the motto has been 'For Excellence We Strive', one of those stirring slogans we old cynics forget as soon as we read it. But in the service area behind the great banqueting rooms, where muted bustle provides unobtrusive service to hundreds of diners, there is a hand-lettered sign stuck up above a doorway, not by the management but by an ordinary member of staff. It simply says:

REMEMBER: For EXCELLENCE we STRIVE.

There are luxury hotels competing with each other in every country, but there is only one Savoy, the *ne plus ultra*. None other has sustained the steady excellence of The Savoy over a century.

This site on the King's Reach of the Thames, on the bend of the river, has been entertaining travellers for a thousand years, some more willing than others. In 1246 Henry III presented the land, then between the two cities of London and Westminster, to his wife's uncle Peter of Savoy, who had followed Eleanor to England to see what pickings were to be had from her fortunate marriage. The ancient Duchy of Savoy, now divided between France, Switzerland and Italy, had many links with Britain, and the part of London where Peter built his great palace was soon called 'Soffey', or Savoy.

Peter entertained prodigally; perhaps his statue is placed above the stainless steel canopy of the Strand

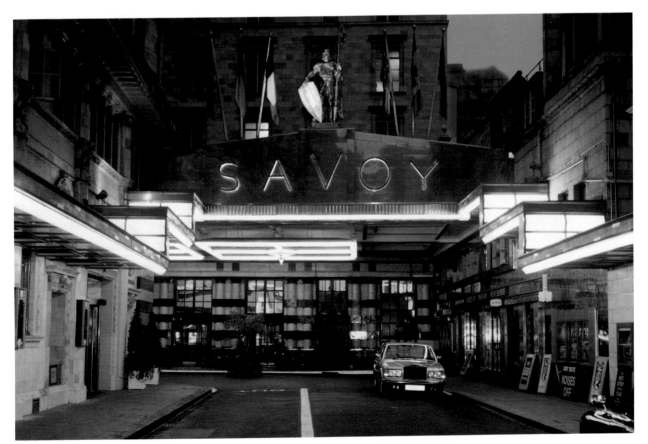

THE FAMILIAR STRAND ENTRANCE TO THE SAVOY

entrance to the hotel as an inspiration to the staff. He went off to recapture Turin from Charles I of Naples in 1266, and was made Prince of Savoy two years later.

The Palace subsequently became the residence of John of Gaunt, Duke of Lancaster, before being burnt down in 1381 during Wat Tyler's insurrection. Still the property of the Duchy of Lancaster, it lay in ruins for a hundred years before a hospice was built on the site. In the seventeenth century the hospice was run by the Jesuits. In the eighteenth century the area became an early example of urban blight and inner

ENGAGING ROOMS BY MARCONIGRAM

city decay; a haunt of thieves, footpads and prostitutes. It was still largely derelict by the time Richard D'Oyly Carte came to build his triumphantly innovative Savoy Theatre in 1881.

Richard D'Oyly Carte was the genius behind The Savoy Hotel. He was primarily a theatrical impresario, the Cameron Mackintosh of his day with Gilbert and Sullivan as his Rice and Lloyd Webber. The trio first collaborated in 1875, achieving instant success, and by 1880 they were making a phenomenal profit of

£60,000 a year. D'Oyly Carte invested his share in the building of the Savoy Theatre, where as well as having the first public building in the world boasting electric lights, he was credited with inventing the queue in order to control the crowds of people trying to get tickets. The invention was successfully exported to countries such as Russia and Poland, but it met with less enthusiasm in France and Italy.

D'Oyly Carte had the Midas touch. With a massive cash surplus, he thought at first of building a block of flats on the rest of the Savoy site, then decided on an hotel. Work began in 1884, and the hotel took five years to build. Looking back from the safety of a hundred years it is difficult for us to grasp how revolutionary the entire concept and execution were.

Thomas Collcutt, who at the same time was designing a huge folly tower at the Imperial Institute in South Kensington, was commissioned as the architect, although Arthur Mackmurdo, who designed the interiors, was originally credited with the work. Architecturally The Savoy was unprecedented. Seven storeys high, it was the first steel-framed building in London as well as the first to use concrete in its construction. Electricity was supplied by its own generating station in the basement and it even had a private artesian well supplying soft water, an unheard-of luxury in London.

D'Oyly Carte demanded perfection. Conscious of the embarrassment of tipping, he also introduced an all-in tariff, with no hidden extras. No Fees! was his slogan in theatre and hotel, and because of The Savoy's modernity he could abolish, as a visiting American approvingly wrote, 'the old hotel notion of extracting payment for the three necessaries of life – baths, lights and attendance'. Two years earlier the Hotel Victoria in Northumberland Avenue had opened in a blaze of publicity with no fewer than four bathrooms between its five hundred guests. The Savoy had seventy bathrooms.

A few hotels in America already had lifts, although they were still very much a novelty, but those at The Savoy were no mere lifts. They were Ascending Rooms, built by the American Elevator Company; spacious, luxurious and panelled in Japanese red lacquer. Lifts meant more profit to the hotelier; previously the more stairs one had to climb, the cheaper

GEORGES AUGUSTE ESCOFFIER

SOUVENIR OF A SUPPER CELEBRATING PUCCINI'S NEW
OPERA MADAM BUTTERFLY AT COVENT GARDEN

the rooms became. An 1893 sales brochure for the hotel tried to put this revolutionary new concept across:

'The hotel is designed to embrace suites of rooms, each suite compact, comfortable and complete in itself. A suite comprises a private sitting room, or rooms, one or more private bedrooms, a private bathroom, lavatory etc. Each set is thus a little home in itself. Those nearest the sky are just as spacious and lofty as those on the ground floor. That is why the charge is the same for a set just under the roof.'

In August 1889 The Savoy opened. London came, and stared, and wondered, and went away again. The hotel was glorious, opulent, magnificent, but it lacked character. D'Oyly Carte recognised the problem: his manager, Mr Hardwicke, did not have the necessary

charisma. He also knew how to solve it and in 1888 he had made an approach to César Ritz, the prince of hoteliers, to ask him to manage the new Savoy. Ritz elegantly declined, preferring the leisured ambience of the resort hotels he had run in Monte Carlo, Baden Baden, Lucerne and San Remo to what he regarded as the cold Calvinistic commercialism of London, at that time the most important city in the world but certainly no tourist centre.

Ritz knew instinctively how to flatter the nobility and the *haut monde* of his time, but like all supreme practitioners of the art of flattery he had no real defence against it when he was the object. D'Oyly Carte tempted him to London to stay in The Savoy as a guest for its opening, on an equal footing with real princes and maharajahs. There he was, this son of a Swiss shepherd from Niederwald, being treated as if he were royalty himself! And like a shepherd's son, he stared at riches unseen before. Never in a life well accustomed to the visual display of affluence had he seen such ostentatious prosperity. Nor was D'Oyly Carte's offer of a lump sum equal to his own annual salary an unacceptable incentive for his advice.

'The wealth and brilliance of London are simply indescribable,' wrote Ritz. London was booming. Incessantly, he began to make notes as to how this aspect of the hotel could be bettered, how that particular service could be improved, how the new-fangled electric light could be shaded to be more flattering to the lady guests, how the cooking by Chef Carpentier in general could never match the standard of one chef in particular. He was lost. The Savoy had claimed him as her own, and D'Oyly Carte had won his most treasured prize, the most renowned hotelier in the world.

Ritz went back briefly to his hotel in Cannes, agog with excitement, before returning to The Savoy. As D'Oyly Carte had anticipated, Ritz brought Autour as his assistant; Agostini as cashier; Echenard, a master of wine, as *maître d'hôtel*; and, of course, Auguste Escoffier, indisputably the world's greatest chef. The arrival of Ritz and Escoffier crowned the glory of The Savoy: within its first year it was recognised as the standard for all hotels to emulate.

Ritz and Escoffier had worked together since 1883, after Ritz had lost his current chef Jean Giroix to another hotel while managing the Grand Hotel Monte Carlo. Like D'Oyly Carte, he knew exactly what he wanted, and acting on Giroix's recommendation he had immediately telegraphed Escoffier to come and join him in Monte Carlo. Together they had created a new style at the Grand, effectively devising the conventions of today's international hotels. Escoffier introduced the *à la carte* menu; waiters were to wear white ties and aprons, station head waiters black ties, and Restaurant Managers morning coats. Nowadays it is all too familiar; then it was an astonishing novelty, the *dernier cri*.

When they came to The Savoy, Britain was regarded as a barbaric outpost in the world of gastronomy. This was partly due to the licensing laws which, although different, were as peculiar then as they are today, and partly due to the dictates of

society. It was not done for a lady to be seen dining in a public place, so hotels and restaurants catered for the gruffer and less refined palates of men, who were more likely to appreciate a healthy faceful of cigar smoke with their 'eternal joints and beefsteaks, boiled fowl with oyster sauce and apple tart' which formed the standard menu of the day.

Escoffier made no secret of the fact that he enjoyed cooking for women, so Ritz set out to alter the custom

THE FRONT COVER OF THE JULY 1906 ISSUE OF 'THE GENTLEWOMAN' DEPICTS THE NEW POPULARITY OF DINING OUT

of centuries. Not only did he succeed in an astonishingly short space of time, he also managed to change British law. With the help of allies and society leaders such as Lady de Grey and Mrs Keppel, it became fashionable for women to frequent The Savoy and subsequently other top class hotels and restaurants.

When the Prince of Wales, later Edward VII, dined at The Savoy with Mrs Langtry it was the ultimate recommendation. As friends of Ritz, Lily Langtry, Lord Randolph Churchill and others lobbied strongly for a change in the licensing laws, which at the time meant that restaurants had to close at 11.00 pm during the week and all day on Sunday. Soon The Savoy Restaurant was open till half past twelve and on Sundays too.

Perhaps this, more than anything, was Ritz's great achievement at The Savoy, in that he changed an entrenched attitude in London society, a society notoriously resistant to change. People began to feel that not only was it socially acceptable to dine at The Savoy, but that it was smarter than dining at home. Nineteen hundred years after the Roman invasion the *passeggio* came to London.

With the passage of time, the name Escoffier has come to sound remote and Olympian, as the great chef has acquired legendary status. Yet the man himself was warm, generous and approachable, modest and restrained in his habits. Like Ritz, he came from peasant stock – he was the son of a blacksmith in Provence – but unlike Ritz, he never acquired a cosmopolitan veneer. Even after ten years in England he could only speak a few words of the language, and was at his happiest when in control of his beloved kitchens. Oddly enough he rarely tasted the dishes he prepared, relying on his remarkable well-developed sense of smell.

Escoffier's true genius lay in his inventiveness. London had never seen or tasted food like his before: *Soufflé d'Ecrevisses à la Florentine; Brochettes d'Ortolan; Pêches à l'Orientale; Canard en Chemise.* All these classic dishes, originated by Escoffier, testify to the man's brilliance. While his talent was acclaimed throughout his working life, his contemporaries esteemed him more for the composition of his menus than for individual dishes.

'Very few people,' wrote Escoffier, 'know what an

THE SUPPER CROWD AT THE SAVOY ARE ENTERTAINED BY
AN EXHIBITION OF THE TANGO

THE FAMOUS
SUPPER SCENE
at
THE SAVOY

At the close of the play—
when notable members
of the dramatic world
and their audiences alike
transfer their thoughts to
the Hotel and Restaurant
—is the moment when
the suggestion of Supper
at the Savoy asserts itself.
Few of the novelties
which have from time to
time swayed the world of
fashion have had more
instant appeal than the
" Tango." Exhibitions of
the facinating innovation
graced many a brilliant
gathering drawn from
both behind and before
the footlights.

arduous task the composing of a perfect menu represents.' Here is one of his menus, from a dinner attended by European royalty on 25th June 1895:

Cantaloup

Consommé à la Française

Velouté à l'Italienne

Truite Saumonée Royale

Paupiettes de Sole aux Fines Herbes

Selle de Pré-salé aux Laitues

Petits Pois Bonne Femme

Suprêmes de Volaille Montpensier

Mousseline à l'Anglaise

Sorbet au Clicquot Rosé

Cailles aux Feuilles de Vigne

Brochettes d'Ortolans

Salade Alexandra

Soufflé d'Ecrevisses à la Florentine

Fonds d'Artichauts à la Moëlle

Pêches Princesse

Biscuit Glacé Savoy

Mignardises

Raisins. Nectarines

Escoffier was also past master at inventing dishes for the many glittering stars who frequented the hotel during the *belle époque*: a brilliant concept which flattered the guest as well as adding glamour and mystique to the dish. He created *Soufflé Tetrazzini* for Luisa Tetrazzini, *Mousseline de Volaille Patti* for Adelina Patti (who was managed by D'Oyly Carte) and, most famously of all, numerous dishes for the great Australian singer Dame Nellie Melba, who actually lived in the hotel for a year.

Sometimes these dishes commemorated particular performances: *Poularde Tosca*, for example, and *Pêches Melba*, originally dreamed up to cap a dinner to celebrate Dame Nellie's performance in *Lohengrin*. *Pêches au Cygne*, as it was first known, was a superb creation: fresh ripe peaches set on a bed of pure vanilla ice-cream, presented on the back of a great swan carved out of a single block of ice and covered with *sucre filé*. It was when Escoffier topped it with a *coulis de framboises* that it became known as *Pêches Melba*. Today, of course, the concoction universally known as Peach Melba – which too often means peaches with ice-

cream and raspberry jam – is a travesty of Escoffier's creation. His actual recipe reads as follows:

'Poach the peaches in vanilla flavoured syrup. Dish them in a timbale upon a layer of vanilla ice-cream, and coat them with a raspberry purée.'

Then there was Melba toast, widely believed to be yet another Escoffier invention for Australia's queen

PROFESSIONAL DANCERS DEMONSTRATE THE LATEST BALLROOM DANCING STEPS

of song: but this was, in truth, a Savoy creation. Madame Ritz inspired it, Ritz suggested the method, Escoffier produced it and called it 'toast Marie' after Madame Ritz – but she modestly passed the honour to Dame Nellie.

For the Prince of Wales, Escoffier devised the extravagantly named *Cuisses de Nymphes à l'Aurore* – Thighs of Dawn Nymphs, in Shakespeare's tongue. The brou-haha when the 'dawn nymphs' proved to be frogs was deafening, but such was the power that the Prince's whims had on society that the following year more frogs' legs were consumed in London than in Paris. Here is the recipe:

'Poach the frogs' legs in an excellent white wine court-bouillon. *When cooled, trim them properly, dry them in a piece of fine linen, and steep them, one after the other, in a* chaud-froid *sauce of fish with paprika, the tint of which*

Untypically for a Frenchman, Escoffier added that frogs were 'the pet abomination of all classes of the population'.

There were equally impressive recipes such as *Pêches au Château Lafite* (simpler, too – 'poach the pea-ches in sufficient Château Lafite to cover them') which, even if you were to use a cooking vintage of Lafite like 1977, would now cost you in the region of £20 worth of wine for each peach. His recipe for *Truffes à la Crème* begins, 'Take 1 lb of truffles. . .'. Truffles today sell in the market at Riberac for £225 a

THE SAVOY ORPHEANS IN THE TWENTIES

should be golden. This done, arrange the treated legs on a layer of champagne jelly, which should have set beforehand on the bottom of a square, silver dish or crystal bowl. Now lay some chervil pluches *and tarragon leaves between the legs in imitation of water-grasses, and cover the whole with champagne jelly to counterfeit the effect of water. Send the dish to the table, set in a block of ice, fashioned as fancy may suggest.'*

kilo, a far cry from Escoffier's days as a conscript at the siege of Metz in the Franco-Prussian war when he noted that truffles were easier to come by than potatoes.

As his wife was not an Anglophile and had not accompanied him to England, Escoffier lived alone at the hotel and poured all his energies into his work. A typical day went as follows:

6.30	Rise, and dress in a severely tailored frock coat. (The chef's toque was only worn on Sundays)
7.00	Inspect the kitchens
8.00	To the office to order food from Covent Garden and Les Halles. Prepare the day's menu. Breakfast in office
9.00	Work in the kitchens. (There was a strict no smoking and no drinking rule)
11.00	To the restaurant to talk with the manager and waiters, to receive and supply details of guests' preferences and dislikes
12.00	Lunch with César Ritz
1.00	To the kitchens
3.30	Office work
4.30	A rapid constitutional; perhaps the chance to visit some suppliers
6.00	Back to the kitchens
9.00	A light solitary dinner
10.00	To the office to write articles and books, and to prepare new menus
12.00	Final tour of the kitchens
00.30	Retire

On Escoffier's instructions, the leftovers from the Restaurant were given to the Poor Sisters of Charity and received by them gratefully; such a gesture would nowadays be considered hopelessly patronising and probably unhygienic to boot.

By the end of the century The Savoy was the world's pre-eminent hotel. It was the focus of London society, then the most glittering anywhere, the place to see and be seen. The cream of Europe and America passed through the white tiled courtyard: royalty and British aristocracy from the Prince of Wales to Lord de Grey and Lord Rosebery; American commercial princes like Vanderbilt and Organ; great European names such as Rothschild and Radziwill, Crespi and Castellane. Monet painted his series of views of the Thames from his room on the fifth floor.

Then in 1897, at the crest of the wave, Ritz resigned. For a lesser hotel it would have been a disaster; The Savoy scarcely faltered, despite the Prince of Wales's much publicised statement 'Where Ritz goes, I go'. The pretext was trifling – a long simmering feud with the housekeeper, Mrs Willis, had boiled into open hostility culminating in Ritz's sudden departure. With him, despite his pleas for them to stay, went his faithful team – including Escoffier.

D'Oyly Carte appeared to face a crisis, but once again his quest for perfection resulted in the ideal successor. No-one else could ever have the charisma of Ritz, but he had floated on an ocean of serenity, buoyed up by his intimates, and outside the charmed

circle, staff turnover was depressingly high. What was needed was not a carbon copy of Ritz, but a new style of management where the ego of the hotelier was subordinate to that of his guests.

D'Oyly Carte knew whom he wanted, but as so often happens the people most in demand were the people most reluctant to move. He bought the Restaurant Marivaux in Paris, and with it Thouraud the chef, and Joseph *le patron*. For a short time they made a team as formidable as Escoffier and Ritz though the style, of course, was different. Whereas Ritz might

GRILL			
Couvert, 6d			
Steak	...	...	1/6
Filet Steak	...	...	2/-
Mixed Grill	...	...	2/6
Grilled and Devilled Bone		...	1/6
Sole	...	... 2/-	3/-
Mutton Chop	...	...	1/6
Pork Chop	...	...	1/6
Mutton Cutlet (1)	...	...	1/-
Lamb Cutlets (2)	...	...	1/6
Kidneys (2)	...	...	1/-
Sausages (2)	...	...	1/-
Rasher of Bacon	...	...	1/-
Pigeon	...	...	3/6
Poulet	...	...from	7/-
Lobster (half)	...	...	2/6
GAME, ACCORDING TO SEASON'S PRICE.			
Cold Lobster (according to size)	...	...	—
Lobster Salad	...	...	2/6
Chicken Mayonnaise	...	...	3/-
Welsh Rarebit	...	...	1/-
Scotch Woodcock	...	...	1/-
Mushrooms 1/-	Baked Potatoes 6d. each.		
Tomatoes	... 9d.		

AN EXTRACT FROM A SUPPER MENU FOR THE SAVOY RESTAURANT IN FEBRUARY 1914

nowadays be regarded as an obsequious snob, Joseph (who, as a Frenchman, always carried a smouldering resentment of his parents for letting him be born in Birmingham) had an altogether more modern approach, and was not above making gentle fun of his high class guests. There is the story of a judge who, on being helped into his coat by Joseph, asked 'How d'ye know it's mine?' 'I don't, milord,' bowed Joseph, a little lower than usual, 'but you gave it to me.'

D'Oyly Carte was in a mood for expansion. With the acquisition of Claridge's in 1893, and the subsequent formation of The Savoy Group, he was looking for a managing director. The perfect candidate was one George Reeves-Smith, then working at the Berkeley, but there was a drawback: he was reluctant to leave. So in 1899 D'Oyly Carte simply bought the Berkeley, and a new captain came on board ship.

George Reeves-Smith, a Yorkshireman, had once

of the copyright of Gilbert and Sullivan productions, widely pirated in that country. He made the most of his time there by staying in the very best hotels and observing the way in which they were run. His plan was to emulate high American standards in Britain with a view to attracting American visitors to his own hotels and making them feel at home there. Never was this policy more fully vindicated than in his creation of the American Bar. When Prohibition was in force in the United States Americans visiting London flocked to The Savoy.

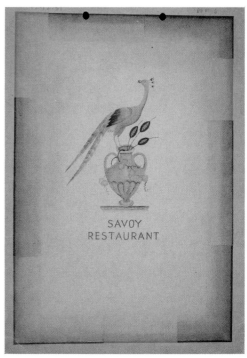

worked as personal assistant to Jean Calvet, the celebrated 'King of Vintners' in Bordeaux, and was acknowledged to be a master of wine when D'Oyly Carte brought him in; but it was not for that quality that he was required. D'Oyly Carte saw in him the administrative flair that the Group would need to maintain its leadership. Although Reeves-Smith was forty when he started at The Savoy, he was to remain at the helm for the next forty years, receiving a knighthood towards the end of his illustrious career.

D'Oyly Carte was an inveterate traveller, particularly to the United States, which he often visited in defence

Harry Craddock, the world's most famous bartender and inventor of the famous White Lady cocktail, presided over the American Bar. Amazingly, Craddock himself was a teetotaller: did he know how good his drinks were? At the very suggestion of a special occasion he would devise a brand new cocktail to mark the event, a custom which The Savoy continues to this day under the direction of the head barman, Peter Dorelli.

Another feature of the American Bar, much appreciated by transatlantic visitors, was its understanding of how Americans like their drinks. Over here we fill the glass with drink, then add ice; over there they fill the glass with ice, then add the drink. It is a simple but

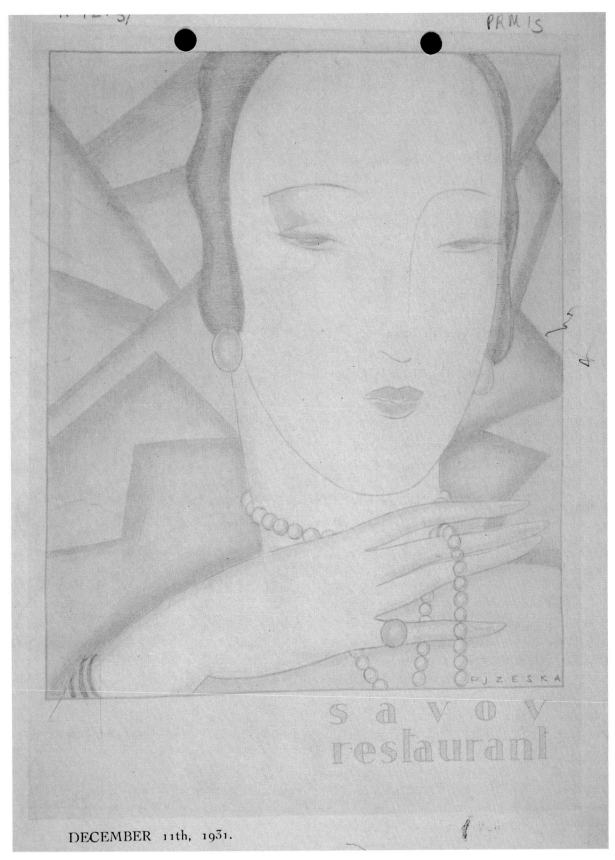

THIRTIES GRAPHICS FROM THE SAVOY ARCHIVES

fundamental difference. The Savoy has always been one of the few establishments in Britain to understand how much ice Americans need in their drinks.

You could say that Harry Craddock effectively ushered in the cocktail age. Before he retired he put his most celebrated concoctions together into a book which became the definitive work on the subject. Early editions of the *Savoy Cocktail Book*, with its jazzy Gilbert Rumbold design epitomising the era, are now highly treasured. The title page describes the work as

> BEING in the main a complete compendium of the Cocktails, Rickeys, Daisies, Slings, Shrubs, Smashes, Fizzes, Juleps, Cobblers, Fixes and other Drinks, known and vastly appreciated in this year of grace 1930, with sundry notes of amusement and interest concerning them, together with subtle Observations upon Wines and their special occasions. BEING in the particular an elucidation of the Manners and Customs of people of quality in a period of some equality.

The book is a gem, with every conceivable kind of cocktail described, and laced with comments drier than a Savoy martini. 'Ladies are advised to avoid this Cocktail as often as possible' is typical of the tome's tone. The Loudspeaker Cocktail 'gives to Radio Announcers their peculiar enunciation. Three of them will produce oscillation, and after five it is possible to reach to osculation stage'. Instructions for the Thunderclap Cocktail are specific: 'Serve, then run for your life!' To the Corpse Reviver (a popular hangover cure) Craddock added the caveat, 'Four of these taken in swift succession will unrevive the corpse again', while the Earthquake Cocktail is 'so-called because if

there should happen to be an earthquake on while you are drinking it, it won't matter'.

———

After the horrors of the Great War those who were left behind played harder, a bright brittle counterpart to the dull muddy thump of the cannon. In the age of the 'flapper' and the Charleston novelty seemed a justification in itself, and no excuse was needed for the most outrageous behaviour or enterprise. Music, and particularly the wireless, was all the rage, and the BBC's predecessor, known as '2LO' gave its first broadcasts from Savoy Hill. The music they played was the sound of the Savoy Orpheans, the hotel's resident band.

Dining to music had for long been an established tradition at The Savoy: the ever-innovative Ritz had started the trend by hiring Johann Strauss, at a phenomenal fee, to 'cover the silence which hangs like a pall over an English dining table'. The habit reached its apogee with the Savoy Orpheans who, at the peak of their popularity in 1924, had a radio audience of 122 million throughout Europe; they were also picked up, via relay stations, across America and even in the Pacific. In the first ten months of their existence, they sold three million gramophone records, at a time when few people possessed the machines on which to play them.

The Savoy Orpheans claimed to be the first international all-star band, and the hotel publicity proudly announced:

'To obtain these ''stars'' 110,000 miles of fruitless journeys were made in searching for and bringing musicians from many parts of Europe and America – several coming from the Pacific coast – for tests and rehearsals.'

The Orpheans described their music as 'symphonised syncopation', and on their first anniversary received messages of congratulations from countless distinguished figures, amongst them Stokowski, Chaliapin and Arnold Bennett. Nearly half a century before we were dazzled by the light shows of Pink Floyd and other mega-bands, the Orpheans were offering fragments of Dvorak's New World Symphony 'with an orchestration of chromatic lighting'.

The Savoy ran several bands in the dancing years – Rudy Vallee joined the Savoy Havana Band in 1924, and in 1926 the popular Carroll Gibbons became leader of the Savoy Sylvians. Gibbons was a prodigiously talented pianist who studied at the Boston Conservatory and gave his first concert at the age of ten; apart from a few short breaks to run HMV's light music division and as MGM's composer in Hollywood, he remained at The Savoy till his tragically early death at the age of 51.

During the twenties and thirties, the *maître-chef* in The Savoy's main restaurant was the Frenchman François Latry, who had come from Claridge's in 1919 (he eventually retired in 1942). Latry coped superbly with the hectic fads and fashions of food through these two troubled decades, and his classic French cuisine had great appeal for American movie stars and British thespians alike – although neither group was averse to teasing the monoglot chef. Asked how he'd like his steak, Tex Austin, the rodeo impresario, drawled: 'Get a bullock, wound it slightly, and drive it in. . .' Bud Flanagan, on being served with a quiche, quipped 'Not Flan again!'

If they preferred, guests could eat in the Grill Room, a quite separate establishment with its own distinct identity. Taking as its motto 'Savoy-fare is savoir-vivre' the Grill Room showed the less formal face of The Savoy, a kind of stars' canteen for the actors at the Savoy Theatre across the courtyard. It attracted a more intimate café society, led by Noel Coward and Gertrude Lawrence, who at one time were permanent fixtures.

The Grill Room had, and has, its own *maître-chef*, a post then held by Jean-Baptiste Virlogeux, a huge, gouty man who was never actually seen to cook anything, but who tasted everything with intensity. In order to provide himself with the imposing sculpted figure that befitted his position, he would encase himself in a vast corset and periodically embark on a spartan *régime* of boiled cabbage, an apple and a glass of milk. After a few week's dieting had made no appreciable difference he would crack and revert to his former gargantuan meals.

By 1930, the exterior of The Savoy had changed

radically, as if anticipating the look of the Thirties. It was then that the extraordinary stainless steel canopy in Savoy Court, designed by architects Easton and Robertson and today the most familar vista of the hotel, first made its dramatic appearance. Underneath was the Savoy Theatre: the old one was demolished in June 1929, to be replaced just 135 days later by a new air-conditioned auditorium with a built-in automatic vacuum cleaner like the hotel. It had been designed by Frank Tugwell and decorated by Basil Ionides, using

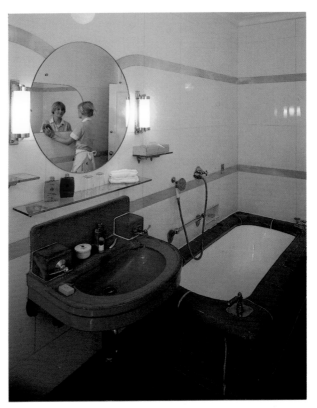

ONE OF THE LEGENDARY BATHROOMS WITH ITS
ORIGINAL FITTINGS BY BASIL IONIDES

five thousand books of silver leaf and two thousand superficial feet of ebony.

But behind all this flamboyance and big spending lay the grim reality of the Depression and the threat of a new war in Europe. The Savoy made a loss for the first time in its history, and it took the early precaution of closing the glass-domed restaurant and moving diners to the relative safety of the basement. Carroll Gibbons, who had been on holiday in America when war broke out, won the hearts of Savoy patrons when he battled through red tape and got back to England to resume his leadership of the Savoy Orpheans, and played through the war.

During and after the war food rationing brought special problems for the Restaurant staff. Although certain commodities remained reasonably plentiful others were in short supply. The professional challenge, for a chef like François Latry who was accustomed to cooking with the best ingredients in the world, lay in finding ways to make appetising and sustaining food out of limited resources. He rose magnificiently to the occasion and devised what was to become his most famous dish. It was to Latry's great credit that the Woolton Pie, named after the Minister for Food and containing potatoes, parsnips, leeks and carrots, became a staple item in most homes.

and a single liqueur and – eh voilà! Until, that is, a Cabinet Minister frowned the practice out of existence.

As for drink, judicious pre-war purchasing had ensured that wines, brandies and liqueurs, although rationed, were not in short supply: at no time was there any serious risk of the cellars running dry. At this time the head cellarman was the extraordinary J. M. Eggle, like Hitler a native of Linz, who seldom stopped work before midnight. He was famous for his mistrust of waiters, saying, 'There is only one difference between a waiter and the devil – a waiter has two tails'.

In the war the American Bar became the unofficial HQ of the U.S. war correspondents, perhaps because

THE SAVOY

has London's most complete Shelter. At night the Restaurant is transferred to the Shelter.

Carroll Gibbons and the Savoy Hotel Orpheans play for dancing, and Vic Oliver appears at midnight.

Arthur Salisbury and his Orchestra play during Dinner.

revised card
22.11.40

THE RIVER ROOM

This room is provided with special protection from blast and splinters. The inner wall is 14 inches thick: the outer wall, five feet distant, is 9 inches thick. The brick joints of each wall are strengthened with steel mesh, and the two walls support each other by 16 connecting steel rods.

There are nine floors of steel construction above the River Room.

The air raid shelter is immediately below.

TWO TABLE CARDS FROM THE SECOND WORLD WAR
REVEALING THE HOTEL'S IMPERTURBABILITY

The usual quota permitted for restaurants was an ounce of meat per diner, and the total bill was not to exceed five shillings. (Before the war a sirloin steak had been four shillings and sixpence and a bottle of vintage Bollinger thirty-five shillings.) Bread was not to be offered unless a diner specifically requested it, a regulation which led to an awkward incident when it was unthinkingly given to some men from the Ministry. But as a designated First Class Establishment the hotel was allowed a little leeway in catering matters. Though *Crêpes Suzette* was a prohibited dish, it was possible for a diner to order a pancake, a single brandy

women were not yet permitted in the bar (a state of affairs not rectified until 1947). The legendary Harry Craddock had retired by then and the journalists called the new barman Vic – well, they *called* him Vic, but his name was actually Johnny Johnson. He was succeeded by Joe Gilmore, who was also known as Vic by the habitués.

Latry retired in 1942, giving way to another Frenchman, Marious Sylvan Dutrey, who achieved the notable feat of securing a reasonable supply of venison and smoked herring from a Scottish contact of Hugh Wontner, Managing Director of The Savoy

Group. Even so, it is said that at one stage Dutrey was seriously contemplating the best way of preparing owl. The following year Camille Payard took over but, sadly, he died of a heart attack in 1946, to be replaced by Auguste Laplanche, a Norman who served The Savoy as *maître-chef* for nearly twenty years.

Working with simple ingredients was less stressful to Laplanche than it had been to Latry, whose instinctive preference was for a more florid style of cookery, but even so, when rationing was finally over, Laplanche used more than a ton of Normandy butter every week, and dishes from Normandy such as *Tripes à la Mode de Caen* and *Canard à la Rouennaise* began to appear on The Savoy's menu. Laplanche's cooking had one particularly distinguished fan – Sir Winston Churchill, who once dined at The Savoy five times in a fortnight. Shortly after the war he also had the honour of cooking for King George VI at the hotel, the first reigning monarch to visit it.

The music played on; Lena Horne sang at The Savoy in the fifties, Josephine Baker in the sixties; and in those Swinging Sixties the hotel became the reluctant centre of press attention when it attempted to hold out against the invasion of the trouser suits. Cathy McGowan, the presenter of ITV's pop programme 'Ready Steady Go!', hit the headlines in 1965 when she was politely turned away from the Restaurant for wearing a trouser suit in the evening. 'We do rather deplore gimmicky clothes,' said a Savoy director, 'particularly with a photographer in the background with the intention of getting a headline.' That was a gauntlet thrown down to Fleet Street, and for five years any self-respecting starlet needing tabloid coverage first attempted to breach the Savoy defences in a trouser suit. Twiggy managed it in 1966 (in orange cords) but it was claimed that the manager had mistaken her for a boy. Lady Whitmore maintained she was the first to be accepted in one, but then attention shifted to men's polo neck shirts, of which Lord Snowdon was a leading exponent. In 1968 the actor David Hemmings was refused admission to the Restaurant because he was wearing a brown corduroy jacket. By 1971 The Savoy's sartorial resistance had crumbled; hot pants were seen in the Grill, although it was still deemed worthy of a press mention.

Within fifteen years guests at a Savoy wedding reception were to gasp at the sight of a stunning pink trouser suit, an exquisite hairstyle, flawless make-up, a jewelled choker at the throat – and that was just the bridegroom. Nick Rhodes, the Duran Duran keyboard player, was getting married in a fantasy of pink. Among the guests were several live flamingos. The tradition of the great Savoy parties lives on: in 1984 Aldo Gucci, whose grandfather had a somewhat different relationship to the hotel, had one of the great rooms converted into a Tuscan grove for his guests,

SIR WINSTON CHURCHILL ACKNOWLEDGING THE CROWDS AS HE ARRIVES AT THE HOTEL FOR A DINNER OF THE OTHER CLUB

who included the Prince and Princess of Wales, Edward Heath and Luciano Pavarotti.

Over the years some rare and wonderful culinary experiments have been carried out in response to guests' wishes. At the Woman of the Year Luncheon in 1964, The Savoy produced a 1,900-year-old recipe for sole with lovage, which they called *Patina Solearum*

Farius Apicius. The hardest task Laplanche had was tracking down the lovage, which he eventually found in a Kentish farm. As Madame Ritz claimed to be the inspiration of Escoffier's *Toast Melba*, so Paolo Contarini, the then general manager, claimed the credit for Laplanche's most astonishing dessert, *Mousse Glacée Cléopatra*. It is a highly elaborate concoction, created for the opening night party of the epic film *Cleopatra* starring Elizabeth Taylor in 1963, and is a dish only a grand hotel could dream of serving:

'For fifteen people, take twelve eggs, separate them and place the yolks with a gill of syrup in a bain-marie at 320°F. Cook them gently till they thicken, then beat till cold and light. Beat the egg whites till stiff, then add sugar and water heated to 240°F and beat again until cold. Add the meringue mixture to the yolk mixture, then beat in a quart of double cream and a quarter bottle of Green Chartreuse until the whole is light and fluffy. Add several ounces of Rosolio liqueur bonbons, pour the mousse into a specially made pyramidal mould, and place in a refrigerator to set. Serve on a silver dish garnished with sliced peaches, strawberries,

raspberries and pineapple covered in Grand Marnier sauce, made from two pounds of apricot sauce, the juice of ten oranges, half a pound of raspberry purée and Grand Marnier liqueur. Top the pyramid with Sauce Chartreuse, made from a pound of apricot sauce, the juice of six oranges and Green Chartreuse.'

On Laplanche's retirement in 1965 Silvino Trompetto, who had been the Grill chef since 1962, took over as the first non-French *maître-chef* at The Savoy. Despite his name, Trompetto had been born in Westminster, of Italian parents. His *Quenelles de Brochet Sauce Bercy* has already reached classic status in international cuisine, likewise his lobster mousse. He canned truffles himself in Madeira wine. Although Savoy cooking has always been predominantly French, English dishes are also available on the menu; Trompetto's Steak and Kidney Pie was a particular favourite, as was his Bread and Butter Pudding. By 1983 the tradition of long service had been re-established, with only two *maître-chefs* since the war. Having achieved the accolade of being the first chef to

THE SAVOY PORTER AWAITS THE ARRIVAL OF
AMERICAN GUESTS AT SOUTHAMPTON DOCKS

receive the MBE, it was time for Trompetto to hand over the ladle to a younger man.

In its hundred year history, the control of The Savoy Group, including Claridge's, The Connaught, The Berkeley, as well as The Savoy itself, has been in the hands of remarkably few men. D'Oyly Carte on his retirement entrusted the Group to George Reeves-Smith. As his own career drew to a close, Reeves-Smith was impressed by the professionalism of a young man named Hugh Wontner. Wontner joined The Savoy in 1938 and when Reeves-Smith retired in 1942, he took over as Managing Director. He successfully took the Group through the war years and was subsequently knighted and became Lord Mayor of London.

When Wontner came to contemplate his own retirement, Giles Shepard was appointed Managing Director of the Group. Like Sir George Reeves-Smith, Shepard had a background in the drinks business. After Eton and the Coldstream Guards, he worked for a brewery and a cider company. It was while he was a director of another hotel, the Dorchester, that Sir Hugh Wontner approached him to talk about the succession. Shepard was flattered and enthusiastic, but his business eye saw that the structure of the Group, while outwardly sound, was not as solid as it could have been.

Bluntly, the hotel was losing money. The standard of service was, as always, impeccable, but in the years that it did not make a loss, the small profits were not a satisfactory return on capital invested. This made the Group vulnerable to predators and Shepard's task was three-fold and immediate: he had to maintain standards, raise profits and fight off unwelcome take-overs. With supreme adroitness he achieved all these aims. The Savoy Group which posted a £1.6 million loss in 1980, made a profit of £12.1 million in 1986. His staff are aware that they work in the world's most famous hotel and they have each acquired a cachet in their varied roles. Under the directorship of Giles Shepard they now have a secure framework in which to perfect their craft.

Behind this great hotel there is also a great woman. Olive Barnett came to work at The Savoy in 1928, and she still visits today to check that the astonishingly high standards she set for her staff are being carried

forward. Miss Barnett, who worked for Sir George and then Sir Hugh as personal assistant, was instrumental in setting up The Savoy's world-famous Professional and Technical Training Department, became the doyenne of the British hotel business, and was awarded the OBE in 1981. She is regarded with affection springing from awe by the world's finest hoteliers. Giles Shepard went on an overseas trip with her shortly after he had been appointed Managing Director in 1979. He was shown to his pleasant but unexceptional room in a grand hotel, then went to

JUDY GARLAND'S CABARET APPEARANCES IN THE FIFTIES ARE STILL REMEMBERED BY GUESTS

collect Miss Barnett for dinner. Her vast, sumptuous suite cascaded with flowers and fruit, her verandah overlooked the most magnificent view, and Shepard realised that as mere Managing Director of The Savoy Group, he would always take second place in the eyes of the hotel manager to the formidable woman who had taught him his trade.

Under Giles Shepard, whose role as The Savoy Group's Managing Director involves responsibility for the group's overall financial interests, there are two figures who are today's equivalent of Ritz and Escoffier. They are the hotel's Managing Director and General Manager Willy Bauer and its *maître-chef* Anton Edelmann, the team who strive tirelessly to maintain the high standards which the Savoy's guests expect. Like many people in the hotel business, both men come from southern Germany, and both are of the opinion that no one has perfected the art of enjoyment like the British upper classes.

Willy Bauer has worked in Britain for twenty-five years. His job, in a nutshell, is to ensure that The Savoy remains the best hotel in the world. The way he achieves this is best summed up by his attitude to his place of work. He used to be assistant manager of a hotel in Swansea. 'It was the best hotel in Wales,' he said. 'I believed it. I felt it. If I thought it was the best, then it had to be the best. Everything I do has to be for the best; it's a policy of perfection – nothing else will do. What is the point in doing something if you don't intend it to be the best you can do?' He works long hours, constantly looking after the needs of the hotel and guests. Three times a day he is seen in the front hall meeting people, and the staff say of him 'he is on stage three times a day and in the wings the rest of it'.

It was Sir Hugh Wontner who gave Bauer the most demanding job briefing imaginable when he was appointed Managing Director – demanding, but short: 'Never compromise.' He accepted the brief with enthusiasm. 'A hotel manager is not just a businessman,' he says. 'He is a specialist in food, wine, interior design, housekeeping, public relations, technical service etc – it's a never ending challenge with unlimited potential. Hotel life is exciting! I deal with royalty and the kitchen porter and I enjoy having to deal with problems and make them right.' A youthful fifty, Bauer admires the example of Sir Hugh Wontner, who retired in 1984 but who still comes in to work at the hotel five days a week. But then retirement is inconceivable to both Bauer and Edelmann, today's Savoy team: you might as well ask a bee when it would stop making honey.

From the start The Savoy has been an international hotel; it was inspired in its concept, amenities and service by the pioneer American luxury hotels; in its food by France and the rest of Europe; in its enter-tainment by the best in the world; in its demeanour by the lazy, friendly elegance of the British aristocrat. This spirit of internationalism is one that is proudly maintained by Bauer and his staff today. They are at ease with all nationalities and intend, with the utmost charm, tact and diplomacy, to keep the mix as it is – so the guest in the resplendent costume at the table next to yours could be from Mongolia, Mozambique or Mexico.

Given a certain level of prosperity, the best eating is to be had not by an endless quest for the new and bizarre but in finding the best source of the classic ingredients. In this The Savoy has an unquestioned advantage. A top-class restaurant may do a hundred *couverts* in an evening: The Savoy Restaurant has to equal or better the standard with up to three hundred *couverts*. How many restaurants can boast eighty chefs? Because of this unique combination of quantity and quality The Savoy, untrammelled by accountants bleating about portion control and price purchasing, can and does buy the best meat in the world.

The old xenophobic defence of British cookery was that the basic materials were so fine that they needed little in the way of enhancement, whereas the French had to disguise the inferior quality of their meats with a bewildering diversity of sauces. The fact that The Savoy insists on Scotch beef, English pork and Welsh lamb shows that the legend is half-true. The meal you enjoy at The Savoy will be made from the finest ingredients, and prepared with all the skill and care that has made it renowned for so long.

The main restaurant is stylish and extremely comfortable, with a bandstand and a dance floor in proper Savoy tradition. The bandstand was designed by Carl Toms and Lord Snowdon in 1983, a remarkable construction of chandelier glass and a Portuguese slate floor, with gunmetal and brass columns.

The Grill Room, formerly known as the Café Parisien, still has its own *maître-chef* and kitchens, and the food is, as one might expect, not a whit less fine; the Grill simply provides an alternative to the classic *haute cuisine* of the Restaurant.

Recently even further choice has been provided by the inclusion of a brasserie, 'Upstairs at The Savoy', the brainchild of Willy Bauer. 'Upstairs' – an intriguing name: 'Let me take you to lunch Upstairs at The Savoy!' – is a delicious surprise. On the first floor there used to be a small and very exclusive shopping arcade with tiny boutiques. Bauer's brainwave was to convert this arcade into a brasserie, and to commission David Mlinaric to design the cool and sophisticated room, with a Cruvinet machine so that individual glasses of fine wine can be served without the necessity of the bottle being finished at one expensive sitting: it will keep the opened wine in perfect condition for months. Overlooking the hotel's main entrance

A banquet at The Savoy promises to be something special, and it is. The food comes from the Restaurant kitchen, therefore it is under the direction of Anton Edelmann himself. One of the groups that regularly holds banquets at The Savoy is called the Savoy Gastronomes; as its members include managers of luxury hotels all over the world, it would not do to serve anything less than the very best.

Original music scores line the walls of the corridor leading to the Private Rooms, each one of which is named after a Gilbert and Sullivan opera. In 1943, in

CHARLIE CHAPLIN AND HIS WIFE WERE FREQUENT
VISITORS IN POST-WAR YEARS

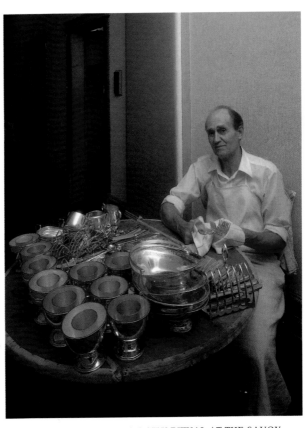

CLEANING SILVER – A DAILY RITUAL AT THE SAVOY

and the Savoy Theatre, one can observe unobserved.

Then there is the banqueting level, which has its own entrance on the Embankment with a distinctive *porte cochère*. The banqueting suites range from luxurious little rooms for an intimate *dîner à deux* to the opulence of the enormous Lancaster Room, formerly known as the Ballroom (the original courtyard of the hotel when the main entrance was in Savoy Hill). Five hundred can dine there in comfort.

the room called 'Patience', Benelux was created by the Foreign Ministers of Belgium, the Netherlands and Luxembourg: the first successful attempt to provide a customs-free trading area in Europe.

The Other Club, founded in 1911 by Winston Churchill and Lord Birkenhead, consists of thirty members, half politicians, half scholars and lawyers. Once a month they still dine at The Savoy, usually in the Pinafore Room, where Kaspar sits on a shelf.

HOW THE GLORIOUS TWELFTH WAS CELEBRATED IN 1987

Kaspar is a black wooden cat carved in 1926 by Basil Ionides, who designed the decor for the Savoy Theatre. If there is a party of thirteen, Kaspar has a place set to make up the numbers to fourteen. He disappeared during the war just after a party of RAF officers had dined rather well in the room. When Winston Churchill dined with The Other Club a fortnight later, he noticed its loss. Within a week Kaspar was back, some say all the way from Singapore.

Somehow one remembers chefs of the *ancien régime* as slow, massive and stately; god-like beings inhabiting a boned and rolled world outside the normal dimensions of life. The new chefs are very different. Anton Edelmann is the very model of the modern *maître-chef*

de cuisine, bristling with energy, alert as a hare. Unlike his illustrious predecessors he has no difficulty with the English language, and in a torrent of words pours out his enthusiasm for cooking, for The Savoy, for life.

Edelmann came to England from Munich in 1971 and started at The Savoy under Silvino Trompetto. From the very first day he knew he wanted to be *maître-chef de cuisine* at the most famous hotel in the world, so when he left to pursue his career elsewhere, it was in the certain knowledge that one day he would be back at The Savoy. He has been there for six years now, and he is still dumbfounded by it. 'Nobody would build a hotel like this nowadays. They'd have to be mad to do such a thing, it is not logical, genius is not logical. That's why it's so nice to be a guest here; it is a voyage of perpetual discovery.'

When Edelmann took over, the first project he set

in hand was the total redesign and rebuilding of the kitchens. A temporary kitchen had to be built at a cost of £500,000, while Escoffier's old ovens, which had been in continuous use from 1895 to 1985, were finally mothballed. The new kitchen, on the first floor in order to be right next to the Restaurant, has cost £3.5 million and is not yet, at the time of writing, quite complete, though H.M. Queen Elizabeth, the Queen Mother, visited it on 5th December 1985.

With the air-conditioning on full blast, the temperature in the kitchen, summer or winter, is a steady 80°F (25°C). 'Never have a cold kitchen. Temperature is of the utmost importance. A cold room – even a cold draught – kills the taste. I say the refrigerator is the bane of food taste. Even cold meats should be warmer – just slightly under room temperature, say. Heat brings out the flavour. That's why we cook food.'

Edelmann is in charge of a carefully structured team. There are the *sous-chefs* who keep an eye on day-to-day operations, the *chefs-de-partie* with their own special area of responsibility – Meat and Game, Fish and so on – and they in turn have their own staff of five or six *commis chefs*. He is, however, acutely aware that he is ultimately responsible for every morsel of food that is prepared in the Restaurant kitchen, and he is forever tasting, sampling, smelling, checking.

As a luxury hotel The Savoy has to be able to provide the best of everything. But the best food, Edelmann insists, is not necessarily the rarest or the most expensive. Talking of food spurs this normally animated and enthusiastic man to near messianic heights. There are highly prized foods; there are foods which are difficult or impossible to grow or rear – the truffle, Colette's 'black pearl of gastronomy', has never been successfully cultivated commercially, and because of its rarity must always remain expensive. Some may consider that the truffle is overrated; Edelmann would not agree. 'It is impossible, it is worth all that is said for it, and more!' He dismisses the normal encounter most people have with them – a sliver of tasteless black rubber on top of a pâté – and describes how to treat a truffle properly for the best reward. 'You take the truffle, fresh of course, and you macerate it in vintage port for a few days. The resulting juice is delicious beyond belief, and is used to make sauce of astonishing pungency.'

Supply and demand has its effect on taste, as does food snobbery. Twenty years ago the kiwi fruit was almost unknown in this country; now it is on a par with Black Forest gâteau in the estimation of many gourmets. Edelmann is a supporter of the maligned fruit – a good one, simply peeled and eaten whole, is not only delicious but has one of the highest vitamin C yields of any fruit. The best food, repeats Edelmann, is the freshest. The Savoy uses only fresh food. If you must eat strawberries and raspberries in January, they will be available and they will be fresh, but please do

ANTON EDELMANN

not ask the price. As George Reeves-Smith once said, The Savoy is expensive, but never dear.

Edelmann admits to appreciating his food more when he is under less pressure. Dealing daily with every known luxury foodstuff, it is difficult to imagine what sort of food he could possibly choose as a treat. To many of us a feast would consist of the aristocratic rarities we can seldom afford – caviar, smoked salmon, foie gras, champagne, oysters, fillet steak, lobster – whereas The Savoy sees these daily. So what delicacies can tempt his palate?

THAT'S ENTERTAINMENT IN THE HOTEL BALLROOM:
CYD CHARISSE, GENE KELLY AND FRED ASTAIRE

Novelty is out for a start. As Edelmann points out, anything worth eating has already been discovered. The reason why snail's egg caviar was not a major delicacy until a couple of years ago is simply that it is not that wonderful a taste experience. It is not offered at The Savoy, though if you could not live without it, it would no doubt be procured for you.

True excellence is to be found in the simplest things. Not so long ago Edelmann had a piece of beef, plainly cooked. It was, he says, outstandingly, indescribably glorious: the texture and flavour were, were – he searches for the right words and fails – 'like meaty butter'. Traced to its source, it was a pure bred Angus from the Hebrides, one of only fourteen left. So many Aberdeen Angus are now crossed with Charolais that the true flavour has been extenuated and we forget how superlative it is, until something like that plain piece of beef comes along to jolt our tastebuds out of their complacency.

Complaining that he has little time to eat, Edelmann polishes off a three-course lunch with evident pleasure: quickly, enthusiastically and completely, yet he remains energetically trim. With a minimum of a fourteen-hour working day he has no time to slump in front of a television set for relaxation *à la mode anglaise*, for when he is not at work he sleeps. The thought of this sort of do-nothing lull is unappealing to him; it would mean a double life.

There is an interesting comparison to be drawn between the daily life of two men, Escoffier and Edelmann, doing the same job but separated by a hundred years. Here, in his own words, is Anton Edelmann's day:

6.30   Rise, and the essential cup of tea to start the motor running.
7.00   Drive to The Savoy. Strictly no car phone, but a tape recorder keeps thoughts marshalled, and dictation is done ready for typing. Most of the recipes in this book started this way.
8.00   Another cup of tea, and the morning kitchen inspection. The toque is always worn.
8.45   Meeting with the *chefs de partie* – there are fourteen, each responsible for a group of cooks who specialise in sauces, pâtisserie, entrées, etc. There are now some female chefs at The Savoy – ten years ago Trompetto would rarely allow a woman into his kitchens.
9.00   Checking the day's orders have been correctly fulfilled; administration.
9.45   Savoy Heads of Departments' meeting with Willy Bauer,

the Managing Director and General Manager of the hotel.
10.00   Control and supervise cooking for lunch.
2.00   Prepare the orders for tomorrow's food.
3.00   A quick lunch with three or four of the six *sous-chefs*.
3.30   General administration, menu writing, proof-reading.
5.30   The right stuff. Some actual cooking is done now, although with eighty chefs at work in the kitchens it is sometimes difficult to find a niche.
9.30   Shower and change, leave the hotel.
10.30   Home.

For holidays Edelmann travels – to eat at other restaurants. He went into cooking simply because he loved food, and one regret of his early life was that while training as a cook, there was neither the money nor the leisure to sample other people's cookery. So every year he goes on a busman's holiday around

TELEVISION PERSONALITY MICHAEL PARKINSON IS PRESENTED WITH A SURPRISE BIRTHDAY CAKE MADE BY HIS SON NICHOLAS, AT THAT TIME A YOUNG COMMIS CHEF IN THE GRILL KITCHEN

Europe, putting on two of three kilos of research. Vigorous games of squash and the heat of The Savoy kitchens take it off again soon enough.

Although both Edelmann and Bauer have strong personalities, rather than superimpose them on the character of the hotel, they both feel that they are upholding the tradition of excellence that has characterised The Savoy from the days of D'Oyly Carte and Ritz. Along with the rest of the staff, they also share an unashamed admiration for the skills of everyone else

THE EARLY MORNING ROUND OF THE MEAT BUYER AT SMITHFIELD MARKET

CHAMPAGNE, CHABLIS AND SEAFOOD
UPSTAIRS AT THE SAVOY

on the team. Francis 'Eddie' Edwards, the chief carver at the hotel, recently made an instructional video on carving techniques, and a small party was held to launch it. Later Bauer described the event correctly and formally – Eddie had carved a duck by way of demonstration – but after he had finished his analytical dissection of Eddie's technique, he shook his head slightly and quietly added: 'It was perfection.' His respect was profound. In the hands of Willy Bauer and Anton Edelmann, the quest for excellence continues into the hotel's second century.

A Savoy Day

MORNING WATCH   4–8

The early morning is quiet, but never still. As always, the hotel is full. Some guests are talking to colleagues in Australia and Japan. Others are still celebrating from the night before. Most are sleeping peacefully in their exceptionally comfortable beds, in somnolent ignorance of the fact that their good night's sleep is perhaps due to superb horsehair mattresses manufactured by The Savoy itself in its small factory in Covent Garden. People have been so impressed by the Savoy mattresses that they insisted on buying one (or two), undeterred by the price of £1,000. Down in the front hall a lady serenely polishes the brass full time, five days a week.

As day breaks, the guests stir luxuriously awake. The hotel never sleeps. Down in the kitchen breakfast is being prepared – the best croissants this side of Paris are being baked, the mighty British breakfast is being constructed. Up in the suites the baths fill silently; alas, this is gradually being phased out as distracted guests sometimes forget the water is running and the bath overflows. But no-one can forget the showerheads – ah, the showerheads! A full foot in diameter, the jets come out like rods. It is a massage and a shower at the same time. Whirlpool baths pale into insignificance by comparison.

FORENOON WATCH   8–12

Guests are up and about their business; the day staff have taken over. Underneath the main part of the hotel the service departments are humming with activity. There are two table men, whose sole function

is moving tables. Behind the banqueting rooms, even now busy as tables are moved and cleaners polish in preparation for the lunchtime functions, lies the original entrance to the hotel in Savoy Hill, now only used by royalty, who need inconspicuous access.

One of the least known streets in London is Savoy Way, a public thoroughfare running through the middle of the hotel. The hotel is above, below and on either side of the road. The Flower Department, the Meat Department and the cold store give on to the road, which is usually impassable, being jammed with delivery lorries. Many of the world's leading hoteliers owe their style and knowledge to The Savoy's renow-

WINNER OF A NATIONAL NEWSPAPER BINGO COMPETITION ENJOYING A CHAMPAGNE BREAKFAST

ned five-year management training scheme which starts off with a month in the Meat Department.

AFTERNOON WATCH   12–4

A guest who thinks she is too busy for lunch needs to fax an urgent message to her San Francisco office. Today she has to go down to the ground floor to The Savoy telecommunications bureau off the Thames Foyer which supplies the telephone, telex and telefax service to guests, but by the Centenary 16-channel cable television will be in all the guests' rooms, as well as the facility to interface with their own personal computers world-wide.

Just as guests' preferences used to be kept on orange cards, they are now computerised. The wood panelled Communications Room, like a ship's bridge, has six brass clocks on the wall, showing the time in Paris, Frankfurt, New York, San Francisco, Tokyo and Sydney. On the way back to her room the busy guest passes the Grill, and decides that perhaps she is not that busy after all.

DOG WATCHES 4–8

The ornate mirrors on the walls of the Thames Foyer, once the centre of the main restaurant, were redis-

SIGNED PHOTOGRAPHS COVER A WALL OF THE
PRESS OFFICE

covered while the room was being redecorated with the *trompe l'oeil* mural, painted by Lincoln Taber in 1980. He painted a crumpled tea towel on one wall so realistically that waiters used to try to pick it up. He also added a fly, but so many people tried to swat it that the whole surrounding area became dirty and it had to be painted out.

Preparations begin for the evening's festivities. There is always something being celebrated at The Savoy. Valets on each floor await the guests' calls.

They are always on hand to steam out the creases, or iron them back in. If as a guest you are lucky enough to catch a valet in a quiet moment, ask for a tale or two, but please do not laugh too loudly as you may disturb the other guests. You will hear tales of evening dresses falling into baths twenty minutes before the ball, of distraught dowagers locked in their bathrooms (there are bells to summon help in every room). In each case the guest has been restored to something approaching equilibrium. Very few people are now accustomed to receiving such service at home but The Savoy has a staff-to-guest ratio of three-to-one. The evening dress disaster is not uncommon – it is a well-known traveller's trick to get the creases out of clothes by hanging them in a steamy bathroom – but at The Savoy there is no need because the valets are quicker and better at pressing clothes than anyone else in the world – even a Fortuny gown would pose no problem.

FIRST WATCH 8–12

In the gentlemen's cloakroom a spiral iron staircase leads to the upper room where the top hats were kept. Shortly after the last war a recently ennobled Labour peer, astonished that he never had to produce his ticket before his topper was instantly handed to him, found the reason in a slip inside which read, 'Ugly bugger. Big nose.' There are 120 diners in the Restaurant and 85 *couverts* in the Grill Room. In the River Room a party to relaunch a motoring publisher is being given. The first night of a major new film is to be celebrated in the Lancaster Room. One of the diners in Iolanthe, a private room, looks as if he could be the German Head of State. He is. A flushed young man angrily sends back his second bottle of wine because 'it's corked'. The perfect wine is replaced without demur. Boisterous laughter comes from a table in the Grill Room. An elderly woman eating alone in her room on the fifth floor turns out her light to look out over the Thames in the moonlight and see what Monet saw. Downstairs in the kitchen 800 meals of an uncompromisingly high quality have been served. The flushed young man is in love.

MIDDLE WATCH 12–4

At any time of the day or night someone somewhere in The Savoy will be washing a dish. Now there are mighty industrial machines to do most of the work, but with seven different designs of china and up to twelve thousand separate pieces in each collection to look after, the task is too complex for mere machines. The services are simply called Courtside, Hotelside, Upstairs, Restaurant, Grill, Private Rooms and Banqueting Rooms. Being a dishwasher at The Savoy has some fine precedents – at the turn of the century an immigrant dishwasher called Guccio Gucci was so astounded by the glamour and wealth of the guests that he went home to Florence to manufacture luxury leather goods for them.　　　　　GWYN HEADLEY

ALDO GUCCI, THE PRINCE AND PRINCESS OF WALES AND
WILLY BAUER

LES
HORS-D'ŒUVRE

OMELETTE OTHELLO

OTHELLO OMELETTE

Chaliapin – nicknamed 'Charlie Pine' by Lady Diana Cooper – always had a suite at the Savoy when he was singing at the Royal Opera House in Covent Garden. His charismatic personality endeared him to all the staff, particularly the chef Latry who appropriately christened this omelette Othello. Chaliapin was one of the few guests who dared to walk into the chef's office without warning to share anecdotes and taste new dishes.

Mix together the mayonnaise, tomato ketchup, horseradish, yoghurt and orange juice. Add the chives and

Ingredients
200 ml/7 fl oz mayonnaise (page 199)
100 ml/3½ fl oz tomato ketchup
10 g/¼ oz freshly grated horseradish
100 ml/3½ fl oz natural yoghurt
50 ml/2 fl oz orange juice
10 g/¼ oz freshly chopped chives
Tabasco
120 g/4½ oz white crab meat
50 g/2 oz smoked salmon, cut in julienne
40 g/1½ oz plum tomato fillets, cut in dice
8 eggs
10 g/¼ oz freshly chopped herbs such as tarragon and chervil
40 g/1½ oz unsalted butter
40 g/1½ oz assorted salad leaves
50 ml/2 fl oz salad dressing (page 201)
salt and freshly milled pepper

Serves 4

season with salt, pepper and a dash of Tabasco.

Mix the crab meat with the smoked salmon and tomato, and add a spoonful of the prepared sauce.

Beat the eggs and herbs with salt and pepper and use to make eight small flat egg pancakes, using a little of the butter for each one. Divide the filling between the egg pancakes and fold over in half.

Mix the salad leaves with the salad dressing, season with salt and pepper and arrange some at the top of each plate. Place two filled pancakes in the centre of each plate and pour some sauce over the pancakes.

GOURMET DELIGHT

SHOWN IN ENGLISH
ON SAVOY MENUS

Chop the fillet of beef very finely. Add the egg yolks, onion, capers, gherkin, parsley and anchovies, and mix well. Season to taste with paprika, Tabasco, Worcestershire sauce, brandy, salt and pepper.

Stamp out eight 5-cm/2-inch rounds of bread and fry in half the butter.

550 g / 1¼ lb fillet of beef, trimmed
2 egg yolks
15 g / ½ oz onion, finely chopped
10 g / ¼ oz capers, finely chopped
10 g / ¼ oz gherkin, finely chopped
10 g / ¼ oz parsley, finely chopped
10 g / ¼ oz anchovies, finely chopped
paprika
Tabasco
Worcestershire sauce
brandy
4 slices of bread
40 g / 1½ oz unsalted butter
20 g / ¾ oz Beluga caviar
4 quails' eggs
salt and freshly milled pepper
fresh chive tops
lamb's lettuce

Serves 4

Divide the beef mixture into eight equal portions and mould each to fit a croûte. Garnish four of the beef croûtes with the caviar. Melt the remaining butter and fry the quails' eggs. Use to garnish the remaining beef croûtes. Garnish with fresh chives and lamb's lettuce.

TERRINE
D'HOMARD ROMILLY

LOBSTER TERRINE ROMILLY

2 × 450 g / 1 lb live
Scottish hen lobsters with eggs

1 litre / 1¾ pints vegetable stock
(page 206)

675 g / 1½ lb fish mousse
(page 196)

50 g / 2 oz carrot,
finely diced and blanched

40 g / 1½ oz leek,
finely diced and blanched

10 g / ¼ oz truffle, very finely diced

100 ml / 3½ fl oz double cream

saffron strands

2 whole leeks

100 g / 4 oz spinach leaves,
blanched

40 g / 1½ oz tiny broccoli florets,
blanched

8 cooked langoustine tails

400 ml / 14 fl oz gazpacho coulis
(page 196)

6 cooked lobster claws,
shell removed

50 ml / 2 fl oz Savoy dressing
(page 201)

salt and freshly milled pepper

dried lobster eggs (page 207),
optional

Serves 10

Remove the lobster eggs from under the tail fins. Cook the lobsters, one at a time, in the boiling vegetable stock for 5 minutes. Drain and refresh, reserving the vegetable stock. Carefully remove the shells from the lobster without damaging the tails. Reserve the four lobster claws.

Reserve 100 g / 4 oz of the fish mousse. Pass the lobster eggs through a very fine sieve and add to the remaining fish mousse. Add three-quarters of the diced vegetables and the diced truffle, and mix thoroughly.

Bring the double cream to the boil, add a pinch of saffron strands and simmer until the cream becomes a very dark yellow. Leave to cool, then add the reserved fish mousse and the remaining diced vegetables. Mix well.

Separate the outside layers of the leeks and trim the green parts neatly. Blanch in boiling salted water until tender. Refresh, dry on a kitchen cloth and season with salt and pepper.

Line a 1.5-litre / 2½-pint terrine with clingfilm, then line the base and sides with the leek, allowing some of it to hang over the edges.

Dry the spinach leaves on a kitchen cloth and lay out to the same length as the terrine and about 10-cm / 4-inch wide. Season with salt and pepper. Spread the saffron mousse evenly over the spinach leaves. Place the lobster tails, overlapping the thin ends to one side of the mousse, and roll up to form a neat roulade.

Spoon a 2.5-cm / 1-inch layer of lobster mousse into the prepared terrine, making a slight indentation along the centre. Position the roulade of lobster in the centre of the terrine and just cover with some of the remaining lobster mousse. Arrange the broccoli florets along the centre of the terrine on top of the roulade and position the langoustine tails on either side. Cover with the remaining lobster mousse. Neatly fold the leek over the lobster mousse and cover with clingfilm.

Poach in a bain-Marie at 150°C / 300°F / gas mark 2 for about 55 minutes until just firm. Leave the terrine to rest for about 30 minutes in a warm place.

Cut the terrine in slices and position one in the centre of each plate. Spoon a little of the gazpacho coulis around each portion. Warm all the lobster claws in a little of the vegetable stock and toss in the Savoy dressing. Garnish each portion with a lobster claw and a few dried lobster eggs, if wished.

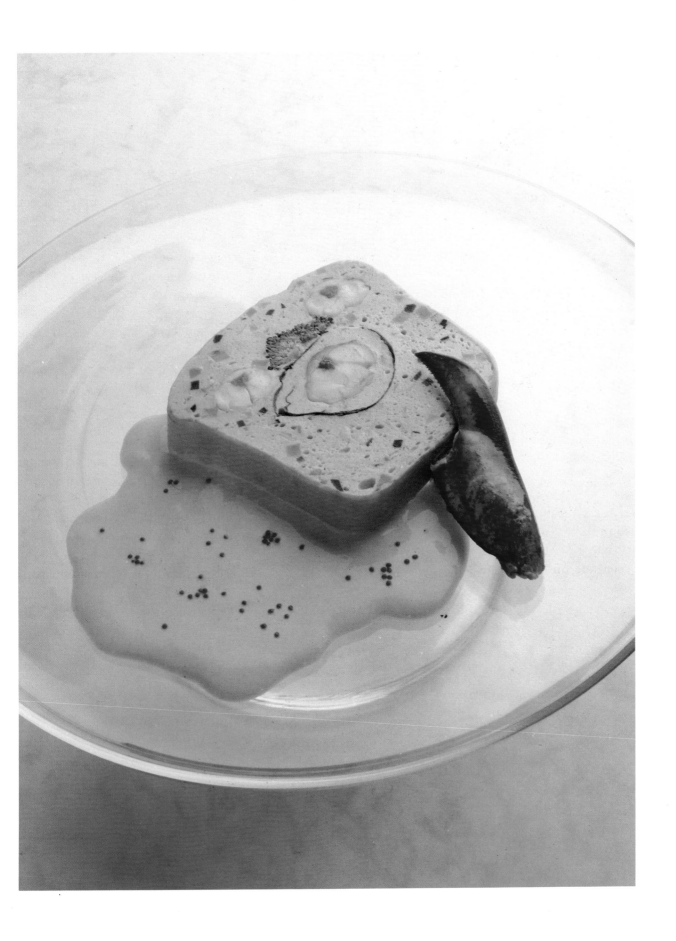

MARBRE DE FOIE DE CANARD ET LANGUE EN GELEE

DUCK LIVER AND VEAL TONGUE PATE IN ASPIC

Cover the raisins with some of the brandy and leave to soak overnight. Drain and reserve any brandy.

Remove the skin and all the veins from the duck liver and cut in 1-cm/ ½-inch thick escalopes. Place the escalopes in a shallow dish and marinate overnight in the port and the remaining brandy with the stick of cinnamon.

Remove the escalopes and dry thoroughly. Reserve the marinade. Season the escalopes generously and quickly seal in a very hot dry pan. Reduce the marinade and any reserved brandy from the raisins by two-thirds and add the Madeira sauce. Continue to reduce to a syrupy consistency. Add the soaked gelatine and the sugar to the warm reduction and season to taste.

Place the veal tongue in cold salted water and bring to the boil. Drain and refresh. Cook the blanched tongue in

20 g/¾ oz raisins
100 ml/3½ fl oz brandy
675 g/1½ lb fresh duck liver
200 ml/7 fl oz ruby port
1 stick of cinnamon
150 ml/¼ pint Madeira sauce (page 198)
2 leaves of gelatine, soaked in a little water
15 g/½ oz sugar
65 g/2½ oz veal tongue
1 onion piqué (page 181)
300 ml/½ pint duck aspic (page 194)
salt and freshly milled pepper
10 tomato roses
20 fresh mint leaves

Serves 10

boiling salted water with the onion piqué until tender. Cool, remove the skin, and cut in 2-cm/¾-inch diameter batons.

Arrange one layer of marinated liver escalopes in a 750-ml/1¼-pint terrine. Brush a thin layer of the syrupy mixture on top and sprinkle with some of the raisins. Continue layering in this way until the terrine is half full. Position a line of veal tongue along the centre of the terrine, then continue layering the escalopes and raisins until the terrine is full. Cover the terrine and weight down. Refrigerate overnight.

Unmould and cut the pâté in thin slices using a warmed knife. Position a slice on each plate. Finely chop the duck aspic and pipe a thin line around each slice of pâté. Garnish each slice with a tomato rose and two mint leaves. Serve with warm miniature brioches.

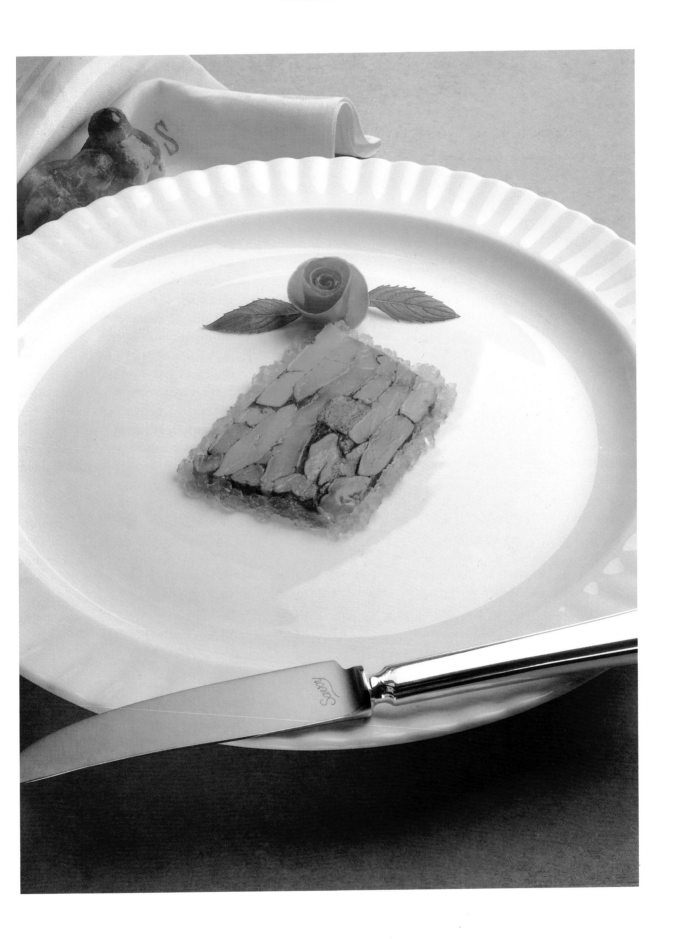

PATE DE CANARD SAUVAGE EN CROUTE FORESTIERE

WILD DUCK PATE IN A PASTRY CASE

3 wild ducks, dressed
1 clove of garlic, chopped
65 g/2½ oz mirepoix (page 207)
24 peppercorns, crushed
1 bay leaf
200 ml/7 fl oz brandy
500 ml/18 fl oz duck stock (page 194)
200 g/7 oz lean pork
250 g/9 oz pork fat
200 ml/7 fl oz ruby port
finely grated rind of 1 orange
50 ml/2 fl oz oil
25 g/1 oz shallot, chopped
50 g/2 oz unsalted butter
25 g/1 oz pistachio nuts, skinned and roughly chopped (page 207)
15 g/½ oz truffle, chopped
675 g/1½ lb paste for pâté en croûte (page 200)
250 g/9 oz barding lard, lightly frozen
150 g/5 oz goose liver pâté
1 egg yolk, beaten
1 litre/1¾ pints duck aspic with port (page 194)
100 g/4 oz assorted wild mushrooms, cleaned
freshly chopped herbs
salt and freshly milled pepper
10 sprigs of mint
10 wild mushroom fleurons (page 206)
200 ml/7 fl oz Cumberland sauce (page 195)
caramelised orange julienne (page 193)

Serves 10

Remove the legs and breasts from the ducks. Remove the bones and all the skin from the legs. Chop all the bones and roast at 220°C/425°F/gas mark 7 for about 20 minutes. Add the garlic, mirepoix, peppercorns and bay leaf. Flame with half the brandy, then add the duck stock and reduce by half, skimming frequently. Pass through a fine sieve.

Cut the meat from the duck legs, lean pork and pork fat in strips. Season with milled pepper, half the port and the orange rind and leave in the refrigerator for about 2 hours. Drain, reserving the marinade.

Finely mince the marinated meats twice, then pass through a fine sieve into a bowl set over ice. Mix well.

Season the duck breasts. Heat the oil and seal very quickly on both sides. Cool and marinate in the remaining brandy and port for at least 4 hours. Drain, reserving the marinade.

Sweat 20 g/¾ oz of the shallots in 15 g/½ oz of the butter, add both marinades and reduce. Add the duck stock and reduce to a glaze. Cool and thoroughly mix into the minced meats. Add the pistachio nuts and truffle, and season generously.

Roll out about three-quarters of the paste to about 3-mm/⅛-inch thick and use to line a 30 × 7.5 × 10.25-cm/ 12 × 3 × 4¼-inch loaf tin, allowing a little to overhang. Cut the barding lard in wafer-thin slices. Line the paste-lined tin, allowing a little to overhang. Pack about one-third of the raw pâté mixture into the tin and position a line of goose liver pâté along the centre. Cover with half the remaining raw pâté mixture and place the duck breasts along the centre. Fill with the remaining raw pâté mixture and fold over the barding lard and paste. Brush the edges with egg yolk.

Roll out the remaining paste about 3-mm/⅛-inch thick and trim to form a lid. Position on top and press the edges of the paste together to seal. Cut out a round opening to allow steam to escape and brush the surface of the paste with egg yolk. Garnish with the remaining paste trimmings and brush with egg yolk. Leave to rest for 20 minutes in the refrigerator. Bake at 220°C/425°F/gas mark 7 for about 15 minutes, then reduce the heat to 180°C/350°F/gas mark 4 and bake for about 25 minutes. The pâté should be slightly pink inside. Leave to cool.

Melt the duck aspic, then leave until cool, but still liquid. Pour into the pâté en croûte through the opening to fill the space between the pâté and the pastry. Refrigerate overnight. Set the remaining aspic, then chop finely.

Sweat the remaining shallot in the remaining butter. Add the wild mushrooms and a sprinkling of fresh herbs. Season to taste.

Cut 1-cm/½-inch thick slices of the pâté. Position one slice on each plate and garnish each portion with chopped aspic, a sprig of mint, a wild mushroom fleuron, wild mushrooms, Cumberland sauce and orange julienne.

PAUPIETTES DE SAUMON FUME FARCIES AU CRABE SAVOY

SMOKED SALMON PARCELS

Mix the crab meat with the diced avocado, cucumber and tomato, and half the salad dressing. Season well with salt and pepper.

Divide the crab meat mixture between the slices of smoked salmon and fold each one into a neat parcel. Arrange two parcels on each plate and top with the caviar. Toss the assorted salad leaves in the remaining salad dressing and season to taste. Arrange on plates and garnish with chive tops.

120 g / 4½ oz white crab meat
20 g / ¾ oz avocado, diced
25 g / 1 oz cucumber, seeds removed and diced
20 g / ¾ oz plum tomato fillet, diced
75 ml / 5 tablespoons salad dressing (page 201)
250 g / 9 oz smoked salmon, cut in 8 thin slices
40 g / 1½ oz Beluga caviar
40 g / 1½ oz assorted salad leaves
salt and freshly milled pepper
chive tops

Serves 4

PETITE SALADE D'HOMARD ET D'ASPERGES

LOBSTER AND ASPARAGUS SALAD

2 × 450 g / 1 lb live Scottish hen lobsters
1 litre / 1¾ pints vegetable stock (page 206)
100 ml / 3½ fl oz walnut oil
25 ml / 1 fl oz tarragon vinegar
caster sugar
16 asparagus tips, cooked
50 g / 2 oz assorted salad leaves
20 g / ¾ oz fresh truffle, thinly sliced
20 g / ¾ oz plum tomato fillets, cut in strips
12 fine green beans, blanched
salt and freshly milled pepper
8 sprigs of chervil

Serves 4

Cook the lobsters in the boiling vegetable stock for 10 minutes. Drain, reserving the stock, and refresh. Remove the shells. Cut both lobster tails into medallions.

Add the walnut oil to the vinegar and whisk continuously until the mixture becomes almost white. Season with sugar, salt and pepper to taste.

Toss the asparagus tips in a little of the walnut dressing, season with salt and pepper and arrange on four plates.

Toss the assorted salad leaves in a little of the dressing and season. Arrange a small amount on each plate.

Gently warm the lobster medallions and claws in the reserved vegetable stock. Drain, then toss in some of the dressing and arrange the medallions and claws on the plates. Garnish with slices of truffle. Season the strips of tomato and green beans, toss in the dressing and arrange around the lobster. Garnish with sprigs of chervil.

PETITE SALADE
DE LANGOUSTINE JAPONAISE

LANGOUSTINE SALAD

Cut the langoustines in half and remove the intestines.

Cook the lentils in boiling salted water until well cooked. Drain and wash under cold running water. Cook the diced vegetables for 1 minute until al dente. Mix the green lentils and diced vegetables with a small amount of Savoy dressing. Season to taste.

Using a mandolin, cut the vegetables in 'spaghetti'. (Use only the green skin of the courgette.)

Cut the streaky bacon in 5-mm/ ¼-inch wide lardons and blanch in boiling water. Refresh and fry until very crisp in the butter.

Mix the langoustines with the vegetable 'spaghetti' and lardons. Toss in a little of the Savoy dressing and season to taste with salt and pepper.

Place some of the green lentil mixture on each plate. Toss the salad leaves in a little of the Savoy dressing, arrange some on each plate and position the langoustine mixture on top. Garnish with sprigs of fennel.

Ingredients
16 cooked langoustine tails (pages 204 and 207)
120 g/4½ oz green lentils, soaked in cold water for at least 4 hours
40 g/1½ oz vegetables such as carrot, leek and celery, diced
50 ml/2 fl oz Savoy dressing (page 201)
40 g/1½ oz carrot
40 g/1½ oz courgette
40 g/1½ oz kohlrabi
40 g/1½ oz streaky bacon
15 g/½ oz unsalted butter
20 g/¾ oz lollo rosso
10 g/¼ oz lamb's lettuce
25 g/1 oz curly endive
salt and freshly milled pepper
4 sprigs of fennel

Serves 4

PRALINE D'OEUF DE CAILLE AU FOIE GRAS

QUAIL'S EGG WRAPPED IN FOIE GRAS

150 g/5 oz Marbré de Canard (page 44)
8 quails' eggs, soft-boiled and shelled (page 207)
40 g/1½ oz young spinach leaves, blanched
10 g/¼ oz hard-boiled egg white fillets, cut in 8 thin strips
4 plum tomato diamonds
300 ml/½ pint duck aspic (page 194)
12 orange segments (page 203)
50 g/2 oz assorted salad leaves
25 ml/1 fl oz orange dressing (page 200)
300 ml/½ pint chicken or vegetable stock (pages 194 and 206)
salt and freshly milled pepper
8 chive tops

Serves 4

Shape a 5-mm/¼-inch thick layer of Marbré de Canard around four of the shelled quails' eggs and refrigerate for about 1 hour.

Thoroughly dry the spinach on a kitchen cloth, remove the stalks and season the leaves. Wrap the pâté balls carefully in the spinach leaves. Garnish each one with two strips of egg white and one tomato diamond. Melt half the aspic and use to coat the pâté balls. Refrigerate the pralines until set. Repeat, if necessary, so they have a shiny coating.

Place one praline on each plate. Finely chop the remaining aspic and pipe a little around the base of each praline. Arrange three orange segments on each plate. Toss the assorted salad leaves in three-quarters of the orange dressing and place at the top of each plate.

Warm the remaining four quails' eggs in the chicken or vegetable stock and dip into the remaining dressing. Place one egg on each salad nest and garnish with chive tops.

SYMPHONIE DE CRUSTACES AUX ŒUFS DE CAILLE

SHELLFISH AND QUAILS' EGGS IN ASPIC

Ingredients
4 fresh oysters, preferably natives
350 ml/12 fl oz dry white wine
10 g/¼ oz shallot, chopped
25 g/1 oz fresh scallop (white part only), cut in thin slices
400 ml/14 fl oz chicken aspic (page 193)
28 plum tomato diamonds
8 truffle diamonds
8 carrot diamonds
8 hard-boiled egg white diamonds
8 leek diamonds
24 sprigs of fresh dill
2 artichoke bottoms, trimmed and cut in 5-mm/ ¼-inch thick slices
20 g/¾ oz cooked lobster tail, cut in 4 medallions
4 cooked langoustine tails
10 g/¼ oz carrot, finely diced and blanched
10 g/¼ oz fennel, finely diced and blanched
10 g/¼ oz leek, finely diced and blanched
4 quails' eggs, soft-boiled and shelled (page 207)
200 g/7 oz cucumber
50 ml/2 fl oz white wine vinegar
25 g/1 oz caster sugar
salt and freshly milled pepper

Serves 4

Wash and open the oysters (page 199). Remove the beards. Bring 100 ml/ 3½ fl oz of the wine to the boil with the shallot. Drop in the oysters and as soon as the liquid returns to the boil, remove the oysters and place in 100 ml/3½ fl oz of cold white wine to cool.

Poach and cool the scallop in the same way. When cold, dry the oysters and scallop thoroughly.

Melt the chicken aspic, then leave to cool. Coat the inside of four dariole moulds with a very thin layer of the aspic. Leave to set in the refrigerator or over a bowl of ice.

Dip the truffle, carrot, hard-boiled egg white, leek and eight of the tomato diamonds in a little aspic and arrange two of each in a star pattern on the base of each mould with a sprig of fresh dill in the centre. Arrange oysters and sliced artichokes on the top of the vegetable diamonds. Pour in a little aspic to just cover and leave to set. Add a little more aspic and swirl around the inside of the moulds.

Arrange the lobster medallions, langoustine tails, scallop, diced vegetables and quails' eggs neatly in the dariole moulds, always lining them with a little aspic and leaving to set between each layer. Cover the last layer with aspic and leave to set in the refrigerator for at least 2 hours.

Canalé the cucumber and cut in very thin slices. Mix the remaining white wine, white wine vinegar, sugar, salt and pepper, and marinate the cucumber slices for 10 minutes. Drain well. Dip the remaining tomato diamonds in the marinade, then drain well. Arrange a neat ring of cucumber slices on each plate.

Unmould a symphonie de crustaces in the centre of each plate. Garnish with the remaining tomato diamonds and sprigs of dill.

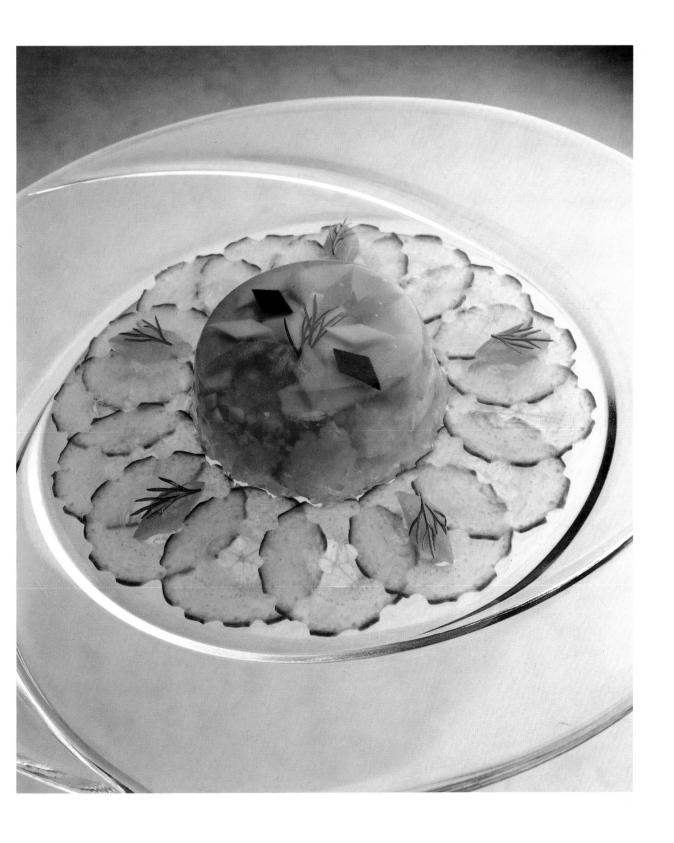

TARTARE DE SAUMON D'ECOSSE A L'ANETH

SALMON TARTARE

Dry the salmon on a kitchen cloth. Mix the salt, sugar and saltpetre. Cover the salmon evenly with this mixture and leave for about 2½ hours. Wash and dry the salmon and leave in a cool place for about 6 hours.

To make the sauce, mix all the ingredients together and whisk until the mixture becomes almost white. Stir in

400 g/14 oz fillet of wild salmon, skin and bones removed
50 g/2 oz sea salt
15 g/½ oz caster sugar
2.5 ml/½ teaspoon saltpetre
juice of ½ lemon
40 g/1½ oz lamb's lettuce
salt and freshly milled pepper
10 g/¼ oz Keta caviar
4 sprigs of dill
SAUCE
150 ml/¼ pint mayonnaise (page 199)
25 ml/1 fl oz white wine vinegar
50 ml/2 fl oz oil
10 g/¼ oz Dijon mustard
50 ml/2 fl oz sugar syrup (page 204)
freshly chopped dill

Serves 4

freshly chopped dill to taste and season with salt and pepper.

Cut the salmon in small cubes and sprinkle with the lemon juice. Arrange the lamb's lettuce and some of the chilled salmon cubes on each plate. Pour a little sauce around each portion and garnish with the caviar and sprigs of dill.

SALADE SAINT-HUBERT

ST HUBERT'S SALAD

Heat the oven to 220°C/425°F/gas mark 7 and roast the grouse for about 10 minutes, the partridge for about 8 minutes and the fillet of venison for about 4 minutes, after which cooking times all the meats will be still be very pink. Leave to rest for 10 minutes in a warm place. Déglacé the roasting tin with the Madeira, reduce and pass through a fine sieve, then add to the Madeira sauce.

Toss the assorted salad leaves in a little orange dressing until just glistening and arrange some in the centre of each plate. Arrange the orange and grapefruit segments around the edge of each portion.

1 grouse, dressed
1 partridge, dressed
100 g/4 oz fillet of venison
100 ml/3½ fl oz Madeira
100 ml/3½ fl oz Madeira sauce (page 198)
75 g/3 oz assorted salad leaves
orange dressing (page 200)
8 segments of blood orange (page 203)
8 segments of orange
8 segments of grapefruit
25 g/1 oz unsalted butter
10 g/¼ oz shallot, chopped
60 g/2½ oz chanterelles, cleaned
freshly chopped chives
25 g/1 oz fresh foie gras, diced
plain flour
25 ml/1 fl oz oil
salt and freshly milled pepper

Serves 4

Remove the breasts from the partridge and grouse and cut in thin slices. Also cut the fillet of venison in thin slices. Arrange some slices of meat on each salad.

Melt the butter and sweat the shallot and chanterelles, season with salt and pepper, sprinkle with a few chopped chives and arrange on top of each portion.

Season the foie gras with salt and pepper and dust very lightly with flour. Heat the oil and very quickly toss the foie gras. Drain and add to the sauce at the last moment; serve this separately in a sauceboat.

TERRINE D'AVOCAT
AUX CRABE ET TOMATES

AVOCADO TERRINE WITH CRAB AND TOMATO

Blanch the spinach quickly in boiling salted water and refresh. Dry thoroughly and season with salt and pepper. Butter a 1.25-litre/2¼-pint terrine and line it with the spinach leaves.

Cut each avocado in half, remove the skin and stone. Reserve two halves and brush with a little lemon juice. Pass the remaining avocados through a fine sieve or blend in a food processor with a little lemon juice.

Warm the gelatine in the chicken stock until dissolved and add the avocado purée. Stir in the crab meat, horseradish and a dash of Tabasco. Fold in the half-whipped cream and season to taste.

150 g/5 oz young spinach leaves

5 medium-sized avocados

juice of ½ lemon

20 g/¾ oz leaf gelatine, soaked in a little chicken stock or cold water

120 g/4½ oz white crab meat

20 g/¾ oz freshly grated horseradish

Tabasco

500 ml/18 fl oz double cream, half-whipped

salt and freshly milled pepper

50 g/2 oz plum tomato fillets, cut in thin strips

75 g/3 oz Keta caviar

50 g/2 oz Beluga caviar

SAUCE

300 ml/½ pint mayonnaise (page 199)

25 ml/1 fl oz white wine vinegar

50 ml/2 fl oz sugar syrup (page 204)

25 ml/1 fl oz Aquavit

150 ml/¼ pint double cream, whipped

10 g/¼ oz freshly chopped chives

Serves 10

Half-fill the lined terrine with the avocado mixture. Cut the reserved avocado in strips and lay along the centre. Cover with the remaining avocado mixture. Fold over any spinach leaves which overlap and chill in the refrigerator for at least 4 hours.

To make the sauce, mix the mayonnaise with the vinegar, sugar syrup, Aquavit and Tabasco to taste. Fold in the whipped cream. Add the chives and season with salt and pepper.

Unmould the avocado terrine and cut in slices about 1-cm/½-inch thick. Position on individual plates and pour a little sauce around each portion. Garnish with tomato fillets and caviar.

VOL-AU-VENT
FINANCIER A LA SAVOY

VOL-AU-VENT WITH KIDNEY AND SWEETBREADS

One of Carême's recipes, this is an example of classic French cooking. It was first made for a member of the Rothschild family – the word financier *in the title subtly suggests the association.*

Roll out the puff paste about 5-mm/¼-inch thick. Cut out four rectangles about 6 × 5-cm/2½ × 2-inch. Mark the top of each rectangle with a knife about 5-mm/¼-inch from the edge and mark a criss-cross pattern in the inner portion.

Place on a baking tray, brush with beaten egg yolk and leave to rest for at least 20 minutes. Bake at 220°C/425°F/gas mark 7 for about 20 minutes until golden brown. Carefully remove the lid from each vol-au-vent and take out any uncooked pastry inside the case.

Melt 25 g/1 oz of the butter in a pan, season the kidneys with salt and

250 g/9 oz puff paste (page 200)
1 egg yolk, beaten
100 g/4 oz unsalted butter
250 g/9 oz veal kidney, fat removed and cut in cubes
225 g/8 oz button mushrooms, cut in quarters
50 ml/2 fl oz truffle juice (page 198)
50 ml/2 fl oz ruby port
50 ml/2 fl oz Madeira
400 ml/14 fl oz jus de veau (page 197)
10 g/¼ oz truffles, chopped
175 g/6 oz veal sweetbreads, blanched and cubed
50 g/2 oz chicken mousse shaped into tiny quenelles (page 206)
40 g/1½ oz fresh cocks' combs, prepared (page 197)
salt and freshly milled pepper
4 turned mushrooms (page 183)
4 slices of truffle

Serves 4

pepper and seal very quickly so that they still remain pink.

Melt 25 g/1 oz of the butter and sweat the mushrooms. Season to taste and remove from the pan. Add the truffle juice, port and Madeira to the pan and reduce by two-thirds. Add the jus de veau and reduce to the desired consistency. Add the chopped truffle, kidneys, sweetbreads, mushrooms chicken quenelles, and cocks' combs. Season to taste and stir in 25 g/1 oz of the butter.

Place a vol-au-vent on each plate and fill generously with the kidney mixture. Melt the remaining butter and brush the vol-au-vent lids with some, then sweat the turned mushrooms in the remaining butter and season to taste. Warm the slices of truffle. Garnish each vol-au-vent with a turned mushroom and a slice of truffle and position the lid.

ASPERGES
AU BEURRE BLANC

ASPARAGUS WITH BEURRE BLANC

Cook the asparagus in boiling salted water for 3–4 minutes until al dente, then refresh. Trim the asparagus to about 10-cm/4-inch in length.

Cut the fillets of salmon and turbot in thin strips about 2-cm/¾-inch wide and 7.5-cm/3-inch long. Wrap the ends of half the asparagus in the salmon and half in the turbot. Warm very quickly in a little vegetable stock until the fish is just cooked. Drain well

Ingredients
16 asparagus spears, peeled
100 g/4 oz fillet of wild salmon, skin and bones removed
100 g/4 oz fillet of turbot, skin and bones removed
300 ml/½ pint vegetable stock (page 206)
4 Timbales d'Asperges (page 186)
200 ml/7 fl oz beurre blanc with lemon (page 192)
12 plum tomato diamonds
15 g/½ oz unsalted butter, melted
salt and freshly milled pepper
16 sprigs of chervil

Serves 4

and dry on a kitchen cloth.

Fan out four asparagus spears on each plate and position one timbale beside the asparagus spears. Warm the beurre blanc and spoon a little over the asparagus.

Season the tomato diamonds with salt and pepper and warm them in the melted butter. Garnish each portion with the tomato diamonds and sprigs of chervil.

OMELETTE ARNOLD BENNETT

ARNOLD BENNETT'S OMELETTE

Arnold Bennett, who wrote Imperial Palace *while he was staying at The Savoy, invented this omelette. He subsequently demanded that chefs made it for him wherever he travelled, so it has now become an international favourite. Not everywhere, however, is it possible to buy the Scottish delicacy finnan haddock, which is always used at The Savoy.*

Poach the haddock in the milk for about 3 minutes. Remove from the pan and flake the fish.

Whisk the eggs, then add salt and pepper and half the haddock.

Heat an omelette pan, add a quarter

Ingredients
300 g / 10 oz smoked finnan haddock fillets
300 ml / ½ pint milk
12 eggs
40 g / 1½ oz unsalted butter
300 ml / ½ pint Béchamel sauce (page 192)
75 ml / 3 fl oz Hollandaise sauce (page 197)
50 ml / 2 fl oz double cream, whipped
20 g / ¾ oz Parmesan, grated
salt and freshly milled pepper

Serves 4

of the butter and swirl around the pan. Add a quarter of the egg mixture and cook very quickly, stirring constantly until the mixture is lightly set. Slide the omelette out on to a plate.

Mix the Béchamel and Hollandaise sauces together quickly. Add the remaining flaked haddock and fold in the whipped cream carefully. Cover the omelette completely with a quarter of the sauce. Sprinkle with a quarter of the Parmesan and glaze under a hot grill.

Repeat with the remaining mixture to make three more omelettes.

Serve immediately.

COQUILLES SAINT-JACQUES GRILLEES SUR CHOU-RAVE, BEURRE AU CITRON VERT

GRILLED SCALLOPS WITH KOHLRABI IN LIME BUTTER SAUCE

Wash the scallops under cold running water and dry on a kitchen cloth. Cut each one in half (page 195).

Reduce the cream, add the vegetable batons, season with salt and pepper and add the Gruyère at the last moment.

Place the shallot, peppercorns, lime juice and white wine in a pan and reduce. Add the vegetable stock and reduce again. Slowly work in 100 g/4 oz of the chilled butter but do not allow to boil again. Pass the sauce through a fine sieve or muslin and season to taste.

10 fresh scallops, with 4 roes reserved
100 ml/3½ fl oz double cream
150 g/5 oz kohlrabi, cut in batons (page 189) and blanched
150 g/5 oz courgettes, cut in batons (page 189) and blanched
25 g/1 oz Gruyère, grated
10 g/¼ oz shallot, chopped
12 peppercorns, crushed
25 ml/1 fl oz fresh lime juice
50 ml/2 fl oz dry white wine
100 ml/3½ fl oz vegetable stock (page 206)
150 g/5 oz unsalted butter, chilled and diced
plain flour
salt and freshly milled pepper
4 sprigs of chervil
dried lobster eggs (page 207), optional

Serves 4

Season the scallops with salt and pepper, then dust each one lightly with flour. Mark a lattice design on each one with red-hot skewers.

Melt the remaining butter and brush the scallops and roes, then grill very quickly on both sides to cook lightly.

Place the vegetable mixture in the centre of each soup plate and glaze lightly under a hot grill. Arrange the scallops and roes on top. Pour the sauce around the scallops and garnish with sprigs of chervil. If wished, a few dried lobster eggs may be sprinkled on the sauce.

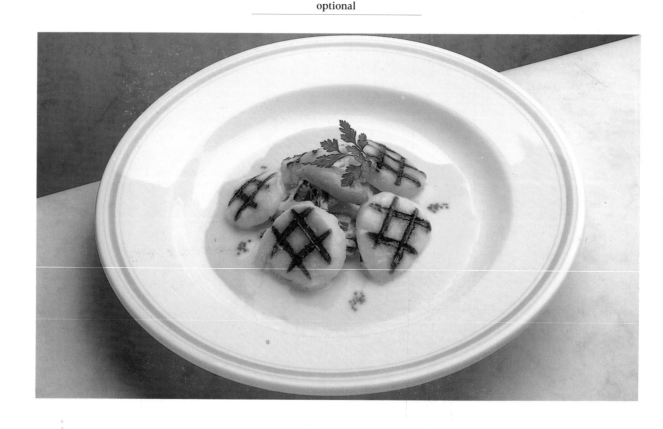

GATEAU DE CAROTTES ET GRUYERE

CARROT GATEAU WITH GRUYERE

Sweat the carrot in half the butter for about 4 minutes. Boil the potato, drain and pass through a fine sieve. Mix the carrot, potato, Gruyère and egg, and season with salt and pepper.

Dust four small buttered cocottes with flour. Fill the cocottes with the vegetable mixture and cover with clingfilm. Steam for about 20 minutes.

Divide the remaining butter and the sugar between two small pans. Glaze

200 g/7 oz carrot, grated
40 g/1½ oz unsalted butter
100 g/4 oz potato
50 g/2 oz Gruyère, grated
1½ eggs, beaten
plain flour
10 g/¼ oz caster sugar
12 baby carrots
12 baby turnips
100 ml/3½ fl oz vegetable stock (page 206)
200 ml/7 fl oz tomato coulis (page 204)
salt and freshly milled pepper
4 sprigs of basil

Serves 4

the baby carrots in one and the baby turnips in the other. Season with salt and pepper. Add half the vegetable stock to each. Cover and cook slowly until al dente.

Warm the tomato coulis. Unmould a carrot gâteau on to each plate. Pour a little tomato coulis around it and position the carrots and turnips. Garnish each portion with a sprig of basil.

FEUILLETE AUX CHAMPIGNONS DE BOIS

WILD MUSHROOMS IN A PUFF PASTRY LEAF

Ingredients
120 g/4½ oz puff paste (page 200)
1 egg yolk, beaten
8 quenelles of game (page 196)
500 ml/18 fl oz chicken stock (page 194)
10 g/¼ oz shallot, chopped
75 g/3 oz unsalted butter
75 g/3 oz ceps, cleaned
75 g/3 oz chanterelles, cleaned
75 g/3 oz pied de mouton, cleaned
freshly chopped herbs such as tarragon, chervil and chives
50 ml/2 fl oz ruby port
100 ml/3½ fl oz jus de veau (page 197)
10 g/¼ oz dried morels, soaked in cold water for at least 1 hour
75 g/3 oz leek, cut in paysanne
salt and freshly milled pepper

Serves 4

Roll out the puff paste 5-mm/¼-inch thick and cut out four large mushroom shapes. Mark with a criss-cross pattern using the back of a knife. Place on a baking tray, brush with egg yolk and leave to rest for at least 20 minutes in a cool place. Bake at 200°C/400°F/gas mark 6 for about 15 minutes until golden brown.

Poach the quenelles very gently in the simmering chicken stock for 8 minutes. Drain and dry on a kitchen cloth.

Sweat the shallot in half the butter until transparent. Add the wild mushrooms to the shallot and sweat for a further 2 minutes. Season with salt and pepper and a sprinkling of herbs.

Reduce the port, add the jus de veau, season with salt and pepper and stir in 15 g/½ oz of the butter. Add the sauce to the mushrooms.

Drain and thoroughly wash the morels. Dry on a kitchen cloth. Melt 15 g/½ oz of the butter, sauté the morels and add to the sauce.

Sweat the leek paysanne in the remaining butter in a covered pan for about 2 minutes until tender. Season with salt and pepper.

Cut the puff pastry shapes in half. Place some leek paysanne on each base and position two game quenelles on top. Spoon some mushroom sauce over each one and top with a puff pastry lid.

RAVIOLI A L'ANCIENNE

RAVIOLI WITH SHELLFISH FILLING

Roll out each noodle paste very thinly and cut each piece in half. On one piece of the beetroot noodle paste position eight small mounds of chicken mousse at regular intervals.

Cut the lobster tail in six medallions. Melt 15 g / ½ oz of the butter and use to toss the medallions. Season to taste and place on top of the chicken mousse. Position a small amount of chicken mousse on top of the lobster. Brush the paste between the lobster with beaten egg and lay the other piece of beetroot paste on top. Press the paste carefully around the filling to seal, then cut in neat squares with a ravioli cutter.

Dry the scallops on a kitchen cloth and season with salt and pepper. Melt 15 g / ½ oz of the butter and use to toss the scallops.

Position eight small mounds of chicken mousse on one piece of the spinach noodle paste at regular intervals, then lay some scallops on top and position a small amount of chicken mousse on the scallops. Brush the paste between the scallops with beaten egg and lay the other piece of spinach noodle paste on top. Press the paste carefully around the filling to seal, then cut with a ravioli cutter.

Add the white crab meat to the

Ingredients
100 g / 4 oz beetroot noodle paste (page 199)
100g / 4 oz spinach noodle paste (page 200)
100 g / 4 oz noodle paste (page 199)
400 g / 14 oz chicken mousse (page 206)
1 × 450 g / 1 lb Scottish hen lobster, cooked for 5 minutes (page 207), shell removed
120 g / 4½ oz unsalted butter
1 egg, beaten
75 g / 3 oz fresh scallops, roes removed and cut in 3-mm / ⅛-inch slices
65 g / 2½ oz white crab meat
20 g / ¾ oz shallot, chopped
12 peppercorns, crushed
100 ml / 3½ fl oz dry white wine
100 ml / 3½ fl oz chicken stock (page 194)
200 ml / 7 fl oz double cream
50 g / 2 oz Roquefort, sieved
basil leaves, cut in julienne
½ clove of garlic, crushed
6 plum tomatoes, filleted and cut in small dice
8 beetroot sulfrino balls, cooked in boiling salted water
12 carrot sulfrino balls, cooked in boiling salted water
12 cucumber sulfrino balls, cooked in boiling salted water
salt and freshly milled pepper
4 sprigs of basil

Serves 4

remaining chicken mousse and position eight small mounds at regular intervals on the noodle paste. Brush the paste between the mousse with beaten egg and lay the other piece of noodle paste on top. Press the paste carefully around the filling to seal, then cut with a ravioli cutter.

Cook all the ravioli in boiling salted water with a dash of oil until al dente. Drain and refresh.

Sweat half the shallots in 15 g / ½ oz of the butter, add the peppercorns and white wine and reduce. Add the chicken stock and cream, and reduce to a thin sauce consistency. Add the Roquefort and season to taste. Stir in a little basil julienne.

Sweat the remaining shallots and garlic in 15 g / ½ oz of the butter until transparent. Add the tomato and simmer until all the liquid has evaporated. Season with salt and pepper.

Place a little tomato in the centre of each plate. Melt 50 g / 2 oz of the butter and toss all the ravioli until warm. Season with salt and pepper and arrange around the diced tomato. Pour a small amount of sauce over each ravioli. Melt the remaining butter and toss the vegetable balls until warm. Garnish the ravioli with sprigs of basil and vegetable balls.

GATEAU DE FOIE BLOND MADAGASCAR

CHICKEN LIVER GATEAU WITH MADAGASCAN PEPPERCORN SAUCE

400 g/14 oz chicken livers, trimmed
500 ml/18 fl oz milk
2 eggs
400 ml/14 fl oz double cream
ground nutmeg
1 red-skinned dessert apple
1 green-skinned dessert apple
50 ml/2 fl oz dry white wine
20 g/¾ oz onion, chopped
50 g/2 oz unsalted butter
25 ml/1 fl oz oil
24 peppercorns, crushed
100 ml/3½ fl oz chicken stock (page 194)
50 ml/2 fl oz jus de veau (page 197)
green peppercorns
freshly chopped basil
salt and freshly milled pepper

Serves 4

Soak the chicken livers overnight in the milk. Drain, wash thoroughly and dry on a kitchen cloth. Finely mince the chicken livers or purée in a food processor, then pass through a fine sieve. Add the eggs and half the cream, and mix well. Season with a little ground nutmeg, salt and pepper.

Line four cocotte dishes with clingfilm, allowing a little to overhang. Fill with the liver mixture, fold over the clingfilm to cover completely and leave to rest in the refrigerator for 30 minutes. Poach in a bain-Marie at 200°C/400°F/gas mark 6 for about 15 minutes. Remove from the oven and leave to rest in a warm place for 10 minutes.

Cut each apple in ten wedges and turn each piece, leaving the skin on one side. Blanch the apples in the wine and refresh. Reserve the wine.

Sweat the onions in half the butter and the oil until transparent. Add the peppercorns and white wine, and reduce. Add the chicken stock, jus de veau and remaining cream. Reduce to the required consistency, then pass through a fine sieve or muslin. Season to taste. Stir in the remaining butter and add a sprinkling of green peppercorns and a little chopped basil.

Unmould a chicken liver gâteau on to each plate. Pour some sauce around each portion and garnish with turned apples.

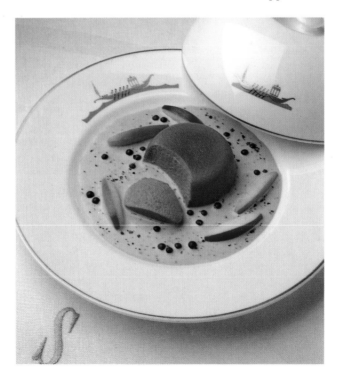

PETIT SOUFFLE D'ASPERGES VERTES
AU BEURRE DE CERFEUIL

**ASPARAGUS SOUFFLE WITH
CHERVIL BUTTER**

Melt 50 g/2 oz of the butter in a saucepan, add the flour and make a roux. Bring the milk to the boil and slowly add to the roux, stirring constantly, to form a smooth sauce. Beat the egg yolks, add to the mixture and cook over a gentle heat for 3–4 minutes, stirring constantly. Add the Gruyère and mustard to taste.

Cook the asparagus in boiling salted water for 3–5 minutes until al dente, then refresh. Cut off the tips about 4-cm/1½-inch in length. Chop the stalks very finely and add to the sauce. Season with salt and cayenne.

75 g/3 oz unsalted butter
40 g/1½ oz plain flour
300 ml/½ pint milk
5 egg yolks
20 g/¾ oz Gruyère, grated
Dijon mustard
75 g/3 oz thin asparagus spears, peeled
cayenne
100 g/4 oz short paste (page 201)
3 egg whites
10 g/¼ oz plum tomato fillets
300 ml/½ pint beurre blanc (page 192)
salt and freshly milled black pepper
8 sprigs of chervil

Serves 4

Roll out the short paste very thinly and use to line four buttered ramekins (about 9-cm/3½-inch in diameter. Whisk the egg whites until very stiff and fold into the warm asparagus sauce with a metal spoon. Use to fill the ramekins. Bake at 200°C/400°F/gas mark 6 for about 25 minutes.

Melt the remaining butter and warm the asparagus tips and tomato fillets. Season to taste. Pour a little of the beurre blanc on to each plate. Unmould the soufflés and place one on each plate. Garnish with asparagus tips, tomato fillets and sprigs of chervil.

MOUSSELINE DE SAINT-JACQUES AUX PERLES D'ESTURGEON

SCALLOP MOUSSELINE WITH CAVIAR

Thoroughly wash and dry the scallop and sole. Season with salt and leave to rest in the refrigerator for at least 20 minutes. Wipe the fish dry again, then mince very finely or work in a food processor.

Set a small bowl in a bowl of ice. Pass the fish mixture through a fine sieve into the chilled bowl. Slowly add the egg white, then slowly stir in the cream, keeping the bowl over ice all the time. Add the egg yolk and season. The consistency should be almost runny at this stage. Leave to rest for 20–30 minutes in the refrigerator until the mousseline mixture becomes slightly firm.

Butter four egg cups or timbales and using a teaspoon, half-fill with the mousseline mixture. Using a teaspoon, form a small cavity in each mousseline

Ingredients
50 g/2 oz fresh scallop (white part only)
25 g/1 oz fillet of sole
½ egg white
100 ml/3½ fl oz double cream
¼ egg yolk
25 g/1 oz Beluga caviar
salt
12 chive tops
SAUCE
10 g/¼ oz shallot, chopped
18 peppercorns
100 ml/3½ fl oz dry white wine
10 ml/2 teaspoons white wine vinegar
10 ml/2 teaspoons double cream
100 g/4 oz unsalted butter, chilled and diced
cayenne

Serves 4

by turning the timbale mould evenly. Fill each cavity with about one-fifth of the Beluga caviar, leaving a little caviar for the sauce. Fill to the rim with the remaining mousseline mixture. Wrap in cling film and steam for exactly 8 minutes. Timing is of the utmost importance in this recipe.

To make the sauce, place the shallots, peppercorns, white wine and white wine vinegar in a saucepan and reduce. Add the cream and reduce again. Slowly work in the diced butter over a very gentle heat. Do not allow the sauce to boil again. Season with cayenne and salt.

Unmould the steamed mousselines on to individual plates. Add the remaining caviar to the sauce at the last moment and pour around the mousselines. Garnish with chive tops.

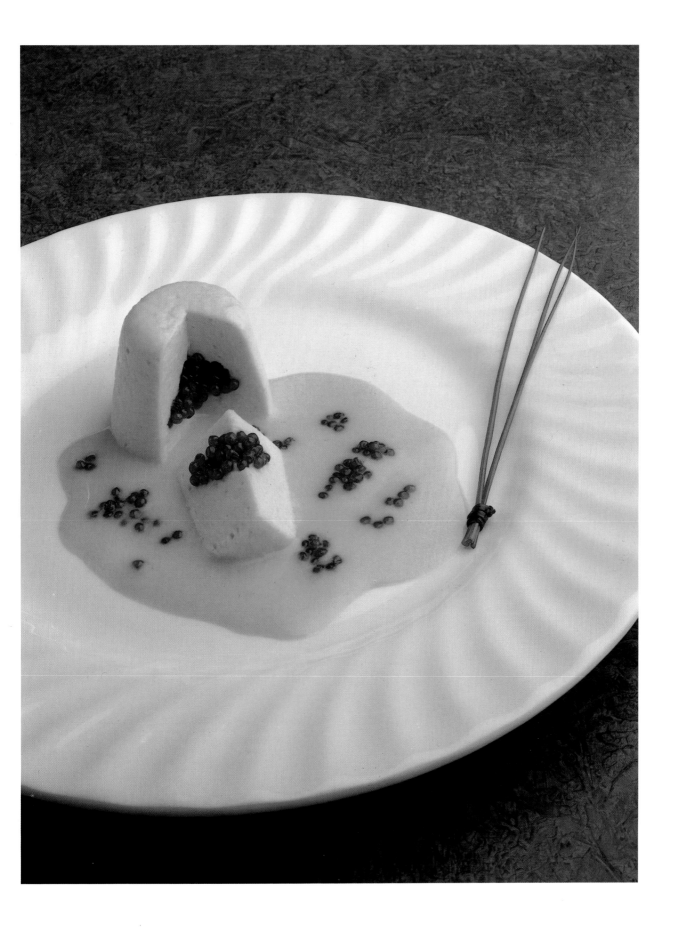

CASSOULET D'ESCARGOTS A L'ANIS

SNAIL CASSEROLE

Sweat the shallot, garlic and diced vegetables in the butter until transparent. Add the snails and chanterelles and flame with the Pernod. Remove the snails and chanterelles, and add the chicken and vegetable stocks. Reduce by half, then add the cream. Reduce again to the desired consistency. Return the snails and chanterelles to the sauce. Add a little freshly chopped fennel and season to taste. Divide the mixture between four small copper skillets or ovenproof dishes.

10 g / ¼ oz shallot, chopped
½ clove of garlic, crushed
20 g / ¾ oz courgette, diced
20 g / ¾ oz carrot, diced
20 g / ¾ oz celeriac, diced
20 g / ¾ oz fennel, diced
20 g / ¾ oz unsalted butter
48 prepared snails (page 207)
100 g / 4 oz chanterelles, cleaned
25 ml / 1 fl oz Pernod
100 ml / 3½ fl oz chicken stock (page 194)
100 ml / 3½ fl oz vegetable stock (page 206)
200 ml / 7 fl oz double cream
freshly chopped fennel
200 g / 7 oz puff paste (page 200)
1 egg yolk, beaten
salt and freshly milled pepper

Serves 4

Roll out the puff paste about 3-mm/ ⅛-inch thick. Stamp out rounds about 2.5-cm / 1-inch larger in diameter than the copper skillets. Brush the edge of the puff paste with egg yolk and use to cover the skillets, pressing the egg-washed paste firmly to the sides of the skillets. Garnish the 'lids' with any puff paste trimmings and brush with egg yolk. Leave to rest for 20 minutes. Bake at 220°C / 425°F / gas mark 7 for 15–20 minutes until the pastry is golden brown.

HUITRES
A MA FAÇON

ANTON EDELMANN'S OYSTERS

24 fresh oysters, preferably natives	
300 ml / ½ pint champagne	
10 g / ¼ oz shallot, chopped	
12 white peppercorns, crushed	
200 ml / 7 fl oz double cream	
25 g / 1 oz carrot julienne, blanched	
25 g / 1 oz leek julienne, blanched	
50 ml / 2 fl oz Hollandaise sauce (page 197)	
cayenne	
salt	
40 g / 1½ oz Beluga caviar	
4 Timbales de Betterave (page 182)	

Serves 4

Wash and open the oysters (page 199), reserve the juice, remove and reserve the beards.

Bring two-thirds of the champagne to the boil and add the shallot and peppercorns. Drop the oysters into the champagne, bring just to simmering point and remove immediately from the pan. Transfer to the remaining cold champagne and leave to cool.

Combine all the champagne with the oyster beards and juice and reduce by half. Pass through a sieve. Add half the cream and reduce to the desired consistency.

Add the julienne of vegetables to the sauce. Whip the remaining cream and add to the sauce with the Hollandaise sauce. Season to taste with cayenne and salt.

Arrange six oysters in a circle and spoon a little sauce over each oyster. Place under a hot grill until golden.

Garnish each oyster with a little caviar and position a timbale in the centre of each plate.

LES
POTAGES

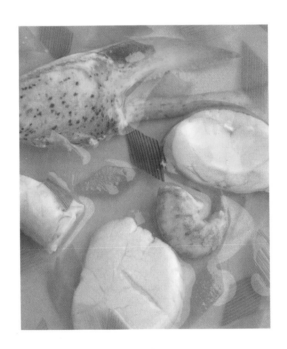

ESSENCE DE POT-AU-FEU CHURCHILL

WINSTON CHURCHILL'S CONSOMME

Sir Winston Churchill insisted that this soup was always served at dinners of The Other Club, of which he was honorary founder. A statue of the distinguished statesman still stands in the Pinafore Room when The Other Club meet. Sir Winston often celebrated his birthday at The Savoy when he would occasionally enjoy two servings of his favourite soup.

Simmer 350 g / 12 oz of the shin of beef in the beef and chicken stocks for about 2 hours until tender. Add the chicken for the last 30 minutes of cooking time. Leave the meats to cool in the stock.

Coarsely mince the remaining shin of beef and mix with the chopped vegetables and egg whites. Add the cooled stock and mix well. Add the thyme, peppercorns, salt and pepper.

Slowly bring to the boil, stirring occasionally with a metal spoon. As

Ingredients
400 g / 14 oz shin of beef
750 ml / 1¼ pints beef stock (page 192)
750 ml / 1¼ pints chicken stock (page 194)
1 small chicken
20 g / ¾ oz onion, chopped
25 g / 1 oz leek, chopped
25 g / 1 oz celery, chopped
25 g / 1 oz carrot, chopped
2 egg whites
1 sprig of fresh thyme
12 white peppercorns
3 young leeks, cooked in stock
120 g / 4½ oz celeriac, turned and cooked in stock
120 g / 4½ oz carrots, turned and cooked in stock
120 g / 4½ oz courgette, turned and cooked in stock
75 g / 3 oz Savoy cabbage balls (page 185)
4 × 2-cm / ¾-inch pieces of marrow bone
½ bread flute
65 g / 2½ oz meat marrow off the bone
20 g / ¾ oz Parmesan, grated
salt and freshly milled pepper

Serves 4

soon as a froth forms on top of the stock, stop stirring and simmer over a very gentle heat for about 2 hours, then pass through fine muslin. Season to taste.

Add the chicken and shin of beef to the consommé. Add the leeks, turned vegetables and Savoy cabbage balls to the soup.

Blanch the pieces of marrow bone for 2 minutes, scrape the bones clean with a knife, then add to the soup. Reheat gently.

Cut the bread flute in thin slices, toast and top with the raw marrow. Sprinkle with Parmesan and brown under a hot grill.

Remove the chicken and beef from the saucepan and cut in slices. Cut the leeks in short lengths. Arrange some of the meat and leeks in each soup plate, ladle some consommé, vegetables and a piece of marrow bone on top and serve the toasted marrow separately.

CREME FINES HERBES
AUX QUENELLES DE STILTON

HERB SOUP WITH STILTON QUENELLES

Serves 4

Pick the herb leaves from their stalks and chop finely. Reserve the stalks.

Sweat the onion in the butter until transparent. Add the fennel, celery and leek to the onion. Sweat for a further 5 minutes. Add 1 litre/ 1¾ pints of the chicken stock, salt, pepper and herb stalks, and simmer for about 20 minutes.

Liquidise, then pass through a sieve and return to the heat. Add the chopped herbs to the soup and simmer for

Ingredients
10 g/¼ oz fresh herbs such as tarragon, fennel, chives, chervil and basil
65 g/2½ oz onion, finely chopped
50 g/2 oz unsalted butter
200 g/7 oz fennel, finely chopped
200 g/7 oz celery, finely chopped
200 g/7 oz leek, white part only, finely chopped
1.5 litres/2½ pints strong chicken stock (page 194)
100 ml/3½ fl oz double cream
200 g/7 oz chicken mousse (page 206)
50 g/2 oz Stilton, cut in dice
20 g/¾ oz vegetables such as leeks and carrots, cut in brunoise and blanched
salt and freshly milled pepper
4 sprigs of basil

about 5 minutes. Whisk in the cream and season to taste.

Mix the chicken mousse, Stilton and vegetable brunoise together and form into twelve quenelles. Poach very gently for about 4 minutes in the remaining stock.

Place three quenelles in each soup plate and ladle some soup over each portion.

Garnish with sprigs of basil and serve with croûtons (page 195).

BISQUE DE LANGOUSTINE AUX RAVIOLI ET CONCOMBRE

LANGOUSTINE BISQUE WITH RAVIOLI AND CUCUMBER

Serves 4

Ingredients
25 ml / 1 fl oz oil
1 kg / 2¼ lb langoustine shells, finely crushed (page 201)
120 g / 4½ oz mirepoix (page 207)
½ clove of garlic, crushed
50 ml / 2 fl oz brandy
40 g / 1½ oz tomato purée
100 ml / 3½ fl oz dry white wine
500 ml / 18 fl oz chicken stock (page 194)
500 ml / 18 fl oz fish stock (page 196)
400 ml / 14 fl oz double cream
100 g / 4 oz noodle paste (page 199)
120 g / 4½ oz fish mousse (page 196)
12 cooked langoustine tails
50 g / 2 oz unsalted butter
1 egg yolk, beaten
40 g / 1½ oz cucumber julienne
salt and freshly milled pepper

Heat the oil and fry the langoustine shells very quickly. Add the mirepoix and garlic and fry for a further 2–3 minutes. Flame with half the brandy, then add the tomato purée. Add the white wine and chicken and fish stocks, and reduce by half. Stir in the cream and reduce to the required consistency. Pass through fine muslin and season the bisque to taste.

Roll out the noodle paste very thinly and cut in half. Divide the fish mousse into eight portions and position four of these evenly spaced on one piece of the noodle paste.

Toss four of the langoustine tails in half the butter, season with salt and pepper, flame with the remaining brandy and place one on top of each portion of fish mousse. Cover with the remaining portions of fish mousse and brush the noodle paste with the egg yolk. Lay the other half of the noodle paste on top and press it carefully around the filling to seal it. Cut into four neat squares with a ravioli cutter. Cook the ravioli in boiling salted water with a dash of oil for 2 minutes.

Toss the cucumber julienne in the remaining butter. Warm the ravioli in the bisque with the cucumber julienne and remaining langoustine tails.

POTAGE DE MOULES ET POIREAUX AU THYM

MUSSEL AND LEEK SOUP

750 g / 1¾ lb fresh mussels
200 g / 7 oz white mirepoix (page 207)
½ clove of garlic
2 sprigs of lemon thyme, stalks and leaves separated
200 ml / 7 fl oz dry white wine
50 g / 2 oz fennel, finely diced
50 g / 2 oz carrot, finely diced
100 g / 4 oz leek, finely diced
65 g / 2½ oz unsalted butter
1 litre / 1¾ pints strong chicken stock (page 194)
saffron strands
200 ml / 7 fl oz double cream
2 egg yolks
50 g / 2 oz plum tomato fillets, finely diced
cayenne
salt

Serves 4

Thoroughly wash and scrub the mussels under cold running water. Ensure they are all firmly closed.

Put the mirepoix, mussels, garlic, stalks of lemon thyme and white wine into a large saucepan. Cover with a lid and cook for 3–5 minutes over a high heat, stirring frequently, until all the mussels have opened.

Strain through a colander into a large bowl, discarding any mussels that remain closed. Cover the mussels with a damp cloth to keep them moist. Place the mussel stock in a tall container tilted at a slight angle to allow any sand to settle. Carefully ladle off the stock from the top.

Remove the mussels from their shells and discard the beards. Sweat the diced vegetables in the butter, add the mussel stock, chicken stock and a generous pinch of saffron, and simmer for about 20 minutes until the vegetables are tender.

Mix the cream with the egg yolks and add some of the hot stock. Add this mixture to the soup and reheat, but do not boil again. Add the mussels, lemon thyme leaves and diced tomato. Season to taste with cayenne and salt.

Serve with warm toasted slices of bread flute.

CRÈME D'HUITRES AU PERNOD

OYSTER SOUP WITH PERNOD

12 fresh oysters, preferably natives
65 g / 2½ oz young spinach leaves, blanched
100 ml / 3½ fl oz dry white wine
25 ml / 1 fl oz Pernod
750 ml / 1¼ pints chicken stock (page 194)
2 egg yolks
200 ml / 7 fl oz double cream
10 g / ¼ oz sorrel, cut in julienne
20 g / ¾ oz carrot julienne, blanched
20 g / ¾ oz leek julienne, blanched
20 g / ¾ oz unsalted butter
cayenne
salt

Serves 4

Wash and open the oysters (page 199). Reserve the juice, remove and reserve the beards.

Remove the stalks and thoroughly dry the spinach on a kitchen cloth. Wrap the oysters in the leaves. Bring the white wine to the boil and cook the oysters for a few seconds. Remove from the pan. Add the Pernod, chicken stock and reserved oyster juice and beards to the wine. Simmer for 3–4 minutes, then pass through fine muslin.

Mix the egg yolks with the cream and add the stock and vegetable julienne. Stir well over a low heat until thickened but do not boil again. Season with cayenne and salt.

Place three prepared oysters in each soup plate and ladle some soup over each portion.

CREME D'OIGNONS AU PORTO

ONION SOUP WITH PORT

Serves 4–6

550 g/1¼ lb onion, finely chopped
65 g/2½ oz unsalted butter
75 g/3 oz fennel, chopped
75 g/3 oz leek, chopped
1 litre/1¾ pints chicken stock (page 194)
100 ml/3½ fl oz double cream
50 ml/2 fl oz ruby port
salt and freshly milled pepper

Sweat the onion in the butter until transparent. Add the fennel, leek, chicken stock, salt and pepper. Simmer slowly for about 25 minutes until all the ingredients are well cooked. Liquidise and pass through a fine sieve. Return to the heat and stir in the cream. Add the port and season to taste.

Ladle the soup into soup plates and garnish with a spoonful of port, if liked. Serve with croûtons (page 195).

ELIXIR DE CRUSTACES EN GELEE

CHILLED CONSOMME WITH SHELLFISH

1 × 450 g/1 lb live Scottish hen lobster
1 litre/1¾ pints vegetable stock (page 206)
4 live langoustines
4 live crayfish
2 fresh scallops, roes removed
100 ml/3½ fl oz dry white wine
100 g/4 oz boned chicken leg meat
1 egg white
20 g/¾ oz celery, chopped
20 g/¾ oz carrot, chopped
10 g/¼ oz onion, chopped
1 litre/1¾ pints chicken stock, chilled (page 194)
saffron strands
15 g/½ oz carrot diamonds, cooked in stock
15 g/½ oz turnip diamonds, cooked in stock
15 g/½ oz leek diamonds, cooked in stock
20 g/¾ oz plum tomato diamonds
salt and freshly milled pepper

Serves 4

Cook the lobster in the boiling vegetable stock for 5 minutes. Drain and refresh. Remove and reserve the shell. Cut the tail in eight medallions.

Cook the langoustines in the boiling vegetable stock for 3 minutes and the crayfish for 2 minutes. Drain and refresh. Remove and reserve the shells.

Cut each scallop in half. Season and poach for 1 minute in the white wine. Leave to cool.

Crush the lobster, langoustine and crayfish shells very finely. Coarsely mince the chicken leg meat. Mix the shells, chicken, egg white, celery, carrot and onion together. Add the chilled chicken stock, a pinch of saffron, salt and pepper, and mix well. Bring slowly to the boil, stirring occasionally with a metal spoon. As soon as a froth forms on top of the stock, stop stirring and simmer over a very gentle heat for 1½–2 hours.

Pass carefully through very fine muslin and season to taste. Chill the consommé until just syrupy.

Divide the lobster claws, medallions, scallops, langoustines, crayfish, vegetable and tomato diamonds between four soup plates and pour the chilled consommé over each portion.

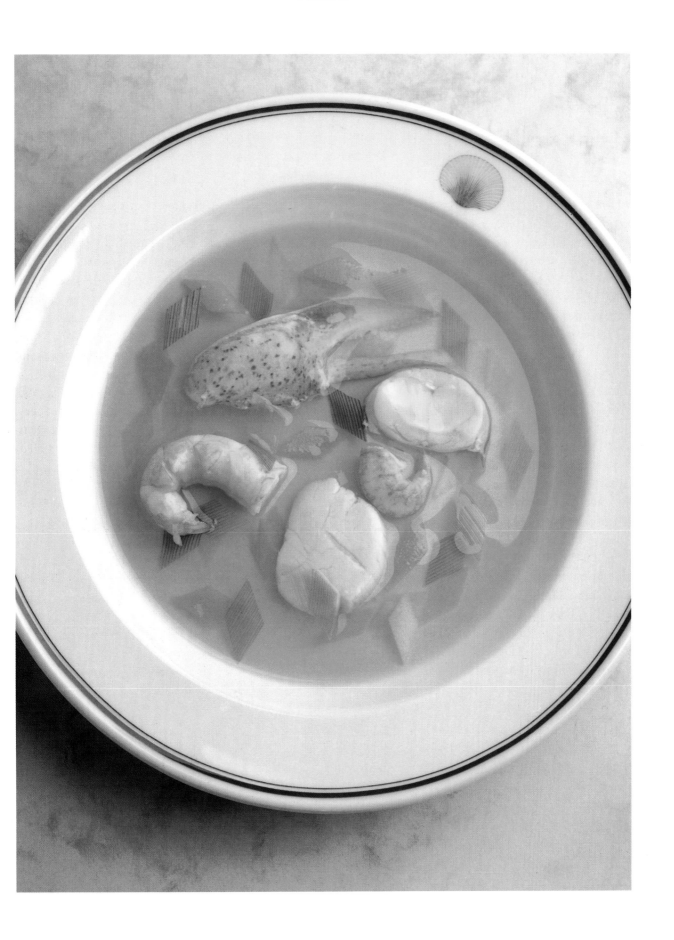

ESSENCE DE CAILLE FUMÉE
AVEC PAILLETTES AU CARVI

SMOKED QUAIL CONSOMME WITH CARAWAY STRAWS

Remove the legs from the quails. Smoke the quail breasts in a hot smoker for 25 minutes. (The breasts are partially cooked in fresh smoke with simultaneous heating in a commercial smoker.) Take the quail breasts off the bone and reserve.

Chop the quails' legs and the smoked quail carcass, and mix with the mirepoix and egg white. Add the cold quail or chicken stock, peppercorns, thyme, bay leaf, salt and pepper. Bring slowly to the boil, stirring occasionally with a metal spoon. As soon as a froth forms on top of the stock, stop stirring and simmer over a gentle heat for about 1 hour. Pass through fine muslin and season to taste.

Cook the vegetable julienne in a little of the quail or chicken consommé for about 2 minutes. Add a sprinkling of freshly chopped herbs to the stuffing, mix well and form into small quenelles using two teaspoons. Poach these in a little of the simmering consommé for about 2 minutes.

2 quails, dressed
40 g/1½ oz mirepoix (page 207)
1 egg white
1.5 litres/2½ pints quail or chicken stock (page 194)
12 peppercorns, crushed
1 sprig of thyme
½ bay leaf
40 g/1½ oz carrot julienne
40 g/1½ oz leek julienne
40 g/1½ oz celery julienne
freshly chopped herbs
20 g/¾ oz stuffing for quail (page 201)
75 g/3 oz puff paste (page 200)
1 egg yolk, beaten
10 g/¼ oz Parmesan, grated
caraway seeds
paprika
4 quails' eggs, soft-boiled and shelled (page 207)
salt and freshly milled pepper
freshly chopped chives

Serves 4

Roll out the puff paste about 3-mm/⅛-inch thick. Brush with beaten egg yolk and sprinkle the paste evenly with the Parmesan, caraway seeds and paprika to taste. Stamp out four rings 2.5-cm/1-inch in diameter. Cut the remaining paste in long strips about 5-mm/¼-inch wide. Roll each strip with your hands working in opposite directions to achieve a twisted straw effect.

Leave to rest for 20 minutes, then bake at 200°C/400°F/gas mark 6 for about 15 minutes.

Cut the caraway straws in 10-cm/4-inch sticks and place four in each pastry ring.

Remove the skin from the smoked quail breasts and cut in slices. Warm the quails' eggs, julienne of vegetable and quenelles in the hot consommé. Arrange one quail breast in each soup plate and ladle some of the consommé over each portion. Garnish with freshly chopped chives. Serve the caraway straws separately.

LES POISSONS ET LES CRUSTACES

TURBOT POCHE AMIRAL

WHOLE POACHED TURBOT

1 × 3.5 kg/8 lb turbot	
400 g/14 oz fish mousse (page 196)	
10 g/¼ oz raw lobster eggs	
2 litres/3½ pints fish stock (page 196)	
2 litres/3½ pints vegetable stock (page 206)	
75 g/3 oz unsalted butter	
1 litre/1¾ pints white wine sauce (page 206)	
cayenne	
10 live crayfish	
10 small button mushrooms, turned	
juice of ½ lemon	
glace de viande (page 197)	
salt and freshly milled pepper	
10 fleurons (page 196)	

Serves 10

The culinary genius of Auguste Escoffier is still venerated by discerning gastronomes. The great chef created this dish when he was introducing the art of haute cuisine to London at the end of the last century. The frequent presence of the Prince of Wales no doubt encouraged society hostesses to start a new custom of entertaining in a public restaurant.

With a long, narrow filleting knife, make an incision at the head end of the backbone and then carefully work down the backbone easing the flesh away without perforating the skin. Turn the fish over and ease the flesh from the other side. Loosen the entire bone and carefully remove from the turbot. Shape ten quenelles from the fish mousse, using two teaspoons, and place on buttered paper.

Pass the raw lobster eggs through a fine sieve and add three-quarters to the remaining fish mousse to colour it. Reserve the remaining quarter for the lobster butter.

Carefully fill the boned-out turbot with the lobster-coloured mousse. It should not be too full as the mousse will expand during poaching.

Place the turbot in a turbotière or a large roasting tin with the dark skin side on top. Season with salt and pepper. Pour in the fish and vegetable stocks. Cover with buttered greaseproof paper and braise at 150°C/300°F/gas mark 2 for about 1 hour, basting frequently with the stock.

Remove the turbot from the tin, reserving the stock. Remove the dark skin very carefully and all the side fins. Dry the fish thoroughly with a kitchen cloth and place on a large silver tray or serving dish.

Mix 50 g/2 oz of the butter with the reserved lobster eggs and chill.

Bring the white wine sauce to the boil, remove from the heat and work in the lobster butter. Season to taste with cayenne, salt and pepper.

Bring some of the reserved stock to the boil and cook the crayfish for 2 minutes, then refresh. With scissors, remove the under-shell from the crayfish tails and loosen the flesh, but do not remove.

Poach the fish quenelles in a little of the reserved stock.

Melt the remaining butter and toss the turned mushrooms. Add a dash of lemon juice to retain the colour.

Arrange the quenelles and button mushrooms along the length of the turbot and pour the sauce carefully over the fish so that it is well covered. Warm the crayfish quickly and arrange around the turbot. Dot the mushrooms with glace de viande. Garnish with the fleurons.

AIGUILLETTES DE TRUITE SAUMONEE ET BARBUE GRILLEES A L'ANETH

GRILLED SALMON TROUT AND BRILL

Cut the fillet of salmon trout in four equal pieces and the fillet of brill in eight equal pieces. Dry each piece on a kitchen cloth. Season with salt and pepper. Dust lightly with flour and mark a lattice design with red-hot skewers on each piece of fish.

Cut the cucumber in 3-mm/⅛-inch thick slices. Reduce the vegetable stock and cream to a very thick consistency. Add the cucumber slices and bring to the boil. Season with salt and pepper and add the diced tomato and a sprinkling of dill at the last moment.

Sweat the onion in half the oil and 15 g/½ oz of the butter until transpar-

200 g/7 oz fillet of salmon trout, skin and bones removed
400 g/14 oz fillet of brill, skin and bones removed
plain flour
400 g/14 oz cucumber, peeled, cut in half lengthways and seeds removed
50 ml/2 fl oz vegetable stock (page 206)
150 ml/¼ pint double cream
20 g/¾ oz plum tomato fillet, diced
freshly chopped dill
65 g/2½ oz onion, finely chopped
25 ml/1 fl oz oil
50 g/2 oz unsalted butter
60 peppercorns, crushed
25 ml/1 fl oz white wine vinegar
100 ml/3½ fl oz dry white wine
200 ml/7 fl oz jus de veau (page 197)
salt and freshly milled pepper
4 sprigs of dill

Serves 4

ent. Add the peppercorns, white wine vinegar and white wine, and reduce. Add the jus de veau and bring the sauce to the boil. Pass through a fine sieve, season to taste and stir in 15 g/½ oz of the butter.

Melt the remaining butter, brush each piece of fish and cook under a medium grill for about 2½ minutes on each side.

Spoon a little cucumber mixture on to each plate. Arrange one piece of salmon trout and two pieces of brill beside it and pour some sauce between the pieces of fish. Garnish with sprigs of dill.

DELICE DE BARBUE BEATRICE

FILLET OF BRILL BEATRICE

300 g / 10 oz potatoes
oil for deep-frying
2 egg yolks
4 × 120-g/4½-oz portions of fillet of brill, skin and bones removed
25 g / 1 oz plain flour
150 g / 5 oz unsalted butter, chilled
50 ml / 2 fl oz oil
8 fresh oysters, preferably natives
100 ml / 3½ fl oz dry white wine
120 g / 4½ oz leek, cut in paysanne
10 g / ¼ oz shallot, chopped
12 white peppercorns, crushed
10 ml / 2 teaspoons lemon juice
50 ml / 2 fl oz vegetable stock (page 206)
50 ml / 2 fl oz fish stock (page 196)
25 ml / 1 fl oz double cream
salt and freshly milled pepper
freshly chopped chives

Serves 4

Cut the potatoes on a mandolin in thin slices, then cut in julienne. Very quickly dip the potato julienne into a deep-fryer of hot oil and blanch them without colouring. Dry on a kitchen cloth and season with salt and pepper. Mix with the egg yolks.

Season the fillets of brill with salt and pepper, dust with flour and cover one side with some of the potato mixture. Heat 50 g/2 oz of the butter and the oil and fry the pieces of fish until golden brown, cooking the potato-covered side first. Remove from the pan and keep warm.

Wash and open the oysters (see page 199). Remove and reserve the beards. Reserve four whole oysters and finely chop the remaining four. Quickly poach the whole oysters in the wine.

Cover and sweat the leeks in 25 g/1 oz of the butter for about 2 minutes until tender. Season with salt and pepper. Place the shallot, pepper corns, wine and lemon juice in a sauce-pan and reduce. Add the vegetable and fish stocks and the oyster beards, and reduce. Add the cream and reduce to the required consistency. Remove from the heat and stir in the remaining chilled butter. Season to taste, then pass through fine muslin. Just before serving, stir in the chopped oysters.

Arrange a little of the leek on each plate and position a fillet of brill on top. Pour a little sauce around each fillet of brill. Garnish each portion with a whole oyster and sprinkle with chives.

HADDOCK FUME ALBAN

ALBAN'S SMOKED HADDOCK

Poach the haddock portions in the milk for about 4 minutes.

Chop the haddock bones, place in a saucepan with the wine, reduce and pass through a fine sieve or muslin. Add the cream to the haddock reduction and reduce to the required consistency. Do not season the cream sauce as the haddock has a high salt content.

Sweat the shallot in half the butter until transparent, add the garlic and sweat for a further 30 seconds. Add the chopped tomato and simmer until all

4 × 100-g/4-oz portions of fillet of smoked haddock, bones removed
400 ml/14 fl oz milk
50 g/2 oz smoked haddock bones
100 ml/3½ fl oz dry white wine
400 ml/14 fl oz double cream
10 g/¼ oz shallot, chopped
20 g/¾ oz unsalted butter
½ clove of garlic, crushed
300 g/10 oz plum tomato fillets, chopped
4 eggs, poached
175 g/6 oz new potatoes, turned and cooked
freshly chopped parsley
salt and freshly milled pepper

Serves 4

the liquid has evaporated. Season with salt and pepper.

Spoon some of the tomato mixture on to each plate and top with a portion of the haddock.

Warm the poached eggs in simmering salted water, then dry on a kitchen cloth. Position a poached egg on each plate and spoon a little sauce over each egg and portion of fish.

Melt the remaining butter and toss the potatoes to warm, sprinkle with a little parsley and position on the plates.

DELICE DE LOTTE
A L'ORANGE

MONKFISH WITH ORANGE SAUCE

8 × 65-g/2½-oz portions of fillet of monkfish

120 g/4½ oz lobster mousse (page 197)

8 large round lettuce leaves

150 ml/¼ pint orange juice

200 ml/7 fl oz white wine sauce (page 206)

40 g/1½ oz unsalted butter

16 orange segments (page 203)

12 green peppercorns

100 g/4 oz beetroot noodles (page 199), cooked

salt and freshly milled pepper

12 chive tops

Serves 4

Dry the monkfish on a kitchen cloth and season with salt and pepper. Top each portion of monkfish evenly with some of the lobster mousse.

Blanch the lettuce leaves in boiling salted water for about 5 seconds and refresh. Dry the leaves on a kitchen cloth and discard the stalks. Wrap the portions of monkfish in the lettuce leaves. Wrap in clingfilm and steam for about 8 minutes.

Reduce the orange juice by two-thirds, add the white wine sauce and season to taste. Stir in half the butter. Add the orange segments and green peppercorns to the sauce.

Toss the noodles in the remaining butter and season with salt and pepper. Arrange some of the noodles in a spiral at the top of each plate.

Remove the clingfilm from the monkfish and position two portions on each plate.

Cover with some of the orange sauce and orange segments. Garnish with chive tops.

MARIAGE DE POISSON
A L'INDIENNE

MARRIAGE OF FISH WITH
A CURRY SAUCE

Carefully remove the scales, then remove any small bones from the red mullet and fillet of salmon with tweezers. Remove the skin from the fillet of salmon and reserve. Cut each scallop in half. Cut the fillet of salmon in strips of the same depth as the scallops and wrap one strip around each piece of scallop. Cut the salmon skin to the same depth as the fillet of salmon and wrap around each piece. Season with salt and pepper.

Mix the fish mousse with a generous sprinkling of fresh herbs, green peppercorns and crab meat. Season generously. Pipe the mixture into a length of sausage skin and tie in small sausages, about 7.5-cm/3-inch long. Simmer in salted water for about 8 minutes. Leave to rest in the refrigerator for at least 4 hours, then remove the skins.

Mark a lattice design with red-hot skewers on each sausage, then warm them in a well-buttered dish at 140°C/275°F/gas mark 1 for 10 minutes.

2 medium-sized red mullet, filleted
50 g/5 oz fillet of salmon
2 fresh scallops, roes removed
250 g/9 oz fish mousse (page 196)
freshly chopped herbs
24 green peppercorns, crushed
10 g/¼ oz white crab meat
a length of sausage skin
50 ml/2 fl oz oil
75 g/3 oz unsalted butter
10 g/¼ oz onion, chopped
½ clove of garlic, chopped
10 g/¼ oz curry powder
20 g/¾ oz plum tomato fillet, chopped
mango chutney
20 g/¾ oz apple, chopped
20 g/¾ oz pineapple, chopped
300 ml/½ pint chicken stock (page 194)
50 ml/2 fl oz white wine sauce (page 206)
50 ml/2 fl oz double cream
100 g/4 oz vegetables such as carrot, kohlrabi and courgette, cut in 'spaghetti' and blanched
salt and freshly milled pepper

Serves 4

Heat half the oil and 25 g/1 oz of the butter and fry the salmon-wrapped scallops on both sides until golden brown.

Season the red mullet with salt and pepper and wrap in clingfilm. Steam for 4 minutes.

Sweat the onions in the remaining oil and 25 g/1 oz of the butter until transparent, add the garlic and sweat for a further 30 seconds. Add the curry powder and sweat for 30 seconds. Add the tomato, a spoonful of mango chutney, the apple, pineapple and the chicken stock, and simmer for about 20 minutes. Liquidise, then pass through a fine sieve. Reduce by two-thirds, add the white wine sauce and double cream, and season to taste.

Toss the vegetable 'spaghetti' in the remaining butter and arrange some on each plate. Position a salmon-wrapped scallop on top and arrange the red mullet and a fish sausage on either side. Pour a little curry sauce around each portion.

DELICE DE TURBOT AU PAMPLEMOUSSE

TURBOT WITH PINK GRAPEFRUIT

4 × 150-g/5-oz portions of fillet of turbot, skin and bones removed
plain flour
150 g/5 oz unsalted butter, chilled
50 ml/2 fl oz fish stock (page 196)
50 ml/2 fl oz vegetable stock (page 206)
12 peppercorns, crushed
10 g/¼ oz shallot, chopped
50 ml/2 fl oz Sauternes
50 ml/2 fl oz pink grapefruit juice
25 ml/1 fl oz double cream
16 green asparagus tips, blanched
12 segments of pink grapefruit
salt and freshly milled pepper
dried lobster eggs (page 207), optional

Serves 4

Dust the portions of turbot with a little flour and mark a lattice design with red-hot skewers. Melt 25 g/1 oz of the butter and brush the fish, season with salt and pepper and cook under a medium grill, design-side down, for 4 minutes. Turn each portion over and brush with more of the melted butter and cook for a further 4 minutes.

Place the stocks, peppercorns, shallot, Sauternes and grapefruit juice in a saucepan and reduce by half. Add the cream and reduce by half. Stir in the remaining butter, reserving 15 g/½ oz. Pass through a fine sieve and season to taste.

Warm the asparagus quickly in the vegetable stock, then toss in the reserved butter and season. Warm the pink grapefruit segments under a medium grill.

Position a portion of turbot on each plate, garnish with asparagus tips and grapefruit segments, pour a little sauce beside each portion and sprinkle with a few lobster eggs, if wished.

FILET DE SAUMON BRAISE AU ROQUEFORT ET CELERI

BRAISED SALMON WITH ROQUEFORT AND CELERY

4 × 150-g/5-oz portions of fillet of salmon, skin and bones removed
150 g/5 oz fish mousse (page 196)
20 g/¾ oz fresh herbs such as chervil and tarragon, finely chopped
25 g/1 oz fresh white breadcrumbs
75 g/3 oz unsalted butter
10 g/¼ oz celery leaves, chopped
300 ml/½ pint white wine sauce (page 206)
20 g/¾ oz Roquefort, sieved
10 g/¼ oz celery julienne, blanched
salt and freshly milled pepper
4 sprigs of celery leaf, deep-fried (page 207)
4 fleurons (page 196)

Serves 4

Season the portions of salmon with salt and pepper. Mix the fish mousse and the herbs, and pass through a fine sieve. Spread a thin layer of the mousse on top of each portion of salmon. Wrap in clingfilm and steam for about 6 minutes.

Remove the clingfilm and sprinkle breadcrumbs over each portion of salmon. Dot each with 15 g/½ oz of the butter and place under a medium grill until brown.

Sweat the chopped celery leaves in the remaining butter, add the white sauce and simmer for about 10 minutes. Liquidise and pass through a fine sieve. Add the Roquefort and celery julienne to the sauce.

Pour a little sauce on to each plate and position a portion of salmon on top. Garnish with deep-fried celery leaves and fleurons.

PAUPIETTES DE SOLE FARCIES D'HOMARD

SOLE PAUPIETTES WITH LOBSTER STUFFING

8 small quarter fillets of sole, skinned and trimmed	
120 g/4½ oz lobster mousse (page 197)	
150 g/5 oz young spinach leaves, blanched and dried	
1 × 450 g/1 lb live Scottish hen lobster	
1 litre/1¾ pints vegetable stock (page 206)	
200 g/7 oz vegetables such as carrot, leek and celeriac, cut in paysanne	
65 g/2½ oz unsalted butter	
50 ml/2 fl oz dry sherry	
200 ml/7 fl oz lobster sauce (page 198)	
25 ml/1 fl oz brandy	
15 g/½ oz dried morels, soaked in cold water for 2 hours	
salt and freshly milled pepper	
2 cooked lobster claws	
4 fleurons (page 196)	
dried lobster eggs (page 207), optional	

Serves 4

Dry the fillets of sole on a kitchen cloth and score the skin side with a small knife. Place between two sheets of plastic and beat lightly. Season each fillet with salt and pepper. Spread a thin layer of lobster mousse on to each fillet of sole and cover the skin side with a layer of dry spinach leaves, then a thin layer of lobster mousse.

Cook the lobster in the boiling vegetable stock for about 5 minutes. Refresh and remove the shell carefully so that the tail and claws remain whole. Cut the lobster tail lengthways into quarters and use with the knuckles to fill the centre of the sole fillets. Roll each one carefully and wrap in clingfilm. Steam for about 8 minutes.

Sweat the vegetable paysanne in 25 g/1 oz of the butter in a covered saucepan. Season and arrange a little on each plate. Remove the clingfilm from the paupiettes of sole and cut each one in three slices. Arrange on the vegetables.

Reduce the sherry, add the lobster sauce and brandy, and season to taste. Stir in 25 g/1 oz of the butter. Pour a little sauce around the paupiettes.

Drain the morels and toss in the remaining butter, season and arrange on the sauce. Warm all the lobster claws in a steamer.

Garnish the paupiettes with lobster claws, fleurons and dried lobster eggs, if wished.

LOUP DE MER
AU CHAMPAGNE EN GONDOLE

SEA-BASS POACHED IN CHAMPAGNE

1 × 1.5 kg / 3 lb sea-bass
60 black peppercorns, very finely crushed
200 ml / 7 fl oz fish stock (page 196)
200 ml / 7 fl oz vegetable stock (page 206)
100 ml / 3½ fl oz pink champagne
12 fresh oysters, preferably natives
10 g / ¼ oz shallot, chopped
25 ml / 1 fl oz double cream
150 g / 5 oz unsalted butter, chilled and diced
small bunch of fresh chives, chopped
cayenne
salt and freshly milled pepper
4 fleurons (page 196)

Serves 4

Open the sea-bass by cutting carefully down either side of the spine. Remove the spine with scissors without damaging the head, tail or belly of the fish. Discard the intestines and wash the body cavity thoroughly. Carefully pull out any small bones with tweezers. Dry the sea-bass on a kitchen cloth.

Place the fish in a buttered ovenproof dish, season with salt and sprinkle generously with the crushed black peppercorns. Pour in the fish and vegetable stocks and champagne. Cover and poach at 180°C / 350°F / gas mark 4 for 12–15 minutes. Remove the sea-bass from the dish and keep covered in a warm place. Reserve the cooking liquid.

Wash and open the oysters. Remove and reserve the beards. Drop the oysters into the cooking liquid for 5 seconds and remove. Keep warm. Add the oyster beards and the shallot to the cooking liquid and reduce. Add the cream and reduce to the required consistency. Remove from the heat and slowly work in the chilled butter. Pass through a fine sieve, but do not boil again. Season to taste. Add the freshly chopped chives and the oysters at the last moment.

Place the sea-bass on a serving dish and spoon over the sauce. Garnish with the fleurons.

DELICE DE FLETAN
AUX POMMES VERTES

HALIBUT WITH APPLE		*Serves 4*

Ingredients:

550 g / 1¼ lb fillet of halibut, skin and bones removed

8 dessert apples, peeled, cored and quartered

75 g / 3 oz unsalted butter

20 g / ¾ oz caster sugar

200 ml / 7 fl oz dry cider

24 fresh basil leaves, cut in julienne

200 ml / 7 fl oz sugar syrup (page 204)

200 g / 7 oz young carrots

10 g / ¼ oz shallot, chopped

12 peppercorns, crushed

100 ml / 3½ fl oz vegetable stock (page 206)

100 ml / 3½ fl oz fish stock (page 196)

300 ml / ½ pint double cream

cayenne

plain flour

salt and freshly milled pepper

4 large sprigs of basil, deep-fried (page 207)

Dry the fillet of halibut on a kitchen cloth, then cut in twelve even slices.

Reserve eight apple quarters, then cut the remainder in small dice. Place a small knob of the butter and the sugar in a pan and melt over a medium heat. Add the apples and 25 ml / 1 fl oz of the cider. Cover with a piece of buttered greaseproof paper and stew very slowly until the apples are soft and the liquid has evaporated. Add half of the basil julienne.

Poach the reserved apple quarters in the sugar syrup for about 1 minute. Drain and place on a baking tray. Brown under a hot grill.

Canalé the carrots and cut in 3-mm / ⅛-inch thick slices. Blanch in boiling salted water, then toss in 15 g / ½ oz of the butter. Season with salt and pepper.

Place the shallots, peppercorns, remaining cider, and vegetable and fish stocks in a saucepan and reduce. Add the cream and reduce to the required consistency. Season with cayenne and salt. Pass through a fine sieve or muslin and stir in 25 g / 1 oz of the butter.

Season the halibut fillets, then dust with flour and sprinkle with the remaining basil julienne. Heat the remaining butter and the oil in a frying pan and cook the pieces of halibut until golden brown on both sides.

Place a 5-cm / 2-inch ring on a plate and fill it to about 1-cm / ½-inch depth with the stewed apple. Repeat three times. Pour a little sauce on to each plate and arrange three pieces of halibut on top. Garnish with apple quarters, carrots and deep-fried basil.

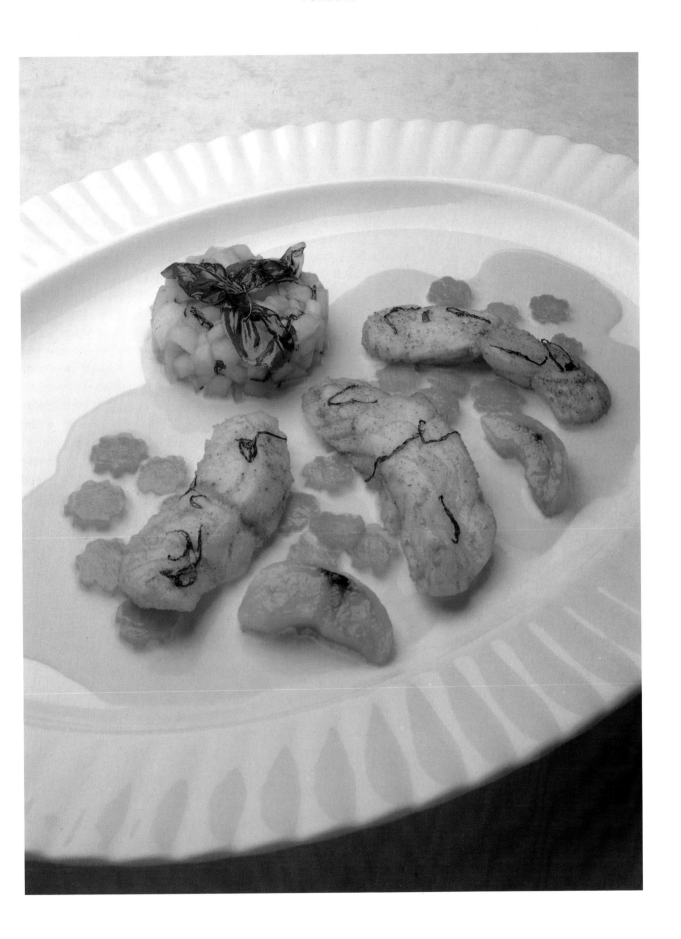

ARLEQUINE DE CRUSTACES ET SA QUENELLE

SHELLFISH IN SAFFRON SAUCE WITH LOBSTER QUENELLE

Ingredients
1 × 450 g / 1 lb live Scottish hen lobster
1 litre / 1¾ pints vegetable stock (page 206), boiling
4 live langoustines
8 live crayfish
120 g / 4½ oz lobster mousse (page 197)
100 ml / 3½ fl oz fish stock (page 196)
100 ml / 3½ fl oz vegetable stock (page 206)
2 fresh scallops, roes removed
100 ml / 3½ fl oz Noilly Prat
20 g / ¾ oz carrot diamonds
20 g / ¾ oz leek diamonds
50 g / 2 oz unsalted butter
10 g / ¼ oz shallot, chopped
12 peppercorns, crushed
200 ml / 7 fl oz double cream
saffron strands
salt and freshly milled pepper
65 g / 2½ oz grapes, peeled

Serves 4

Cook the lobster in the boiling vegetable stock for 5 minutes. Drain and refresh. Cook the langoustines in the boiling vegetable stock for 3 minutes. Drain and refresh. Cook the crayfish in the boiling vegetable stock for 2 minutes. Drain and refresh.

Remove the shell from the lobster and cut the lobster tail in medallions. Remove the shells from the langoustines and the crayfish, then trim the tails (page 204).

Shape the lobster mousse into four quenelles and gently poach in the fish and vegetable stocks for about 5 minutes. Remove from the pan and dry on a kitchen cloth.

Cut the scallops in half and season with salt and pepper. Bring the Noilly Prat to the boil and blanch the scallops very quickly.

Sweat the vegetable diamonds in half the butter in a covered pan until tender. Reduce the Noilly Prat with the fish and vegetable stocks, shallot and peppercorns. Pass through fine muslin. Reduce the cream with a generous pinch of saffron strands and stir in the reduced stock. Add the vegetable diamonds, season to taste and stir in the remaining butter.

Warm the pieces of lobster, langoustines and crayfish very quickly in the sauce, then add the quenelles and scallops. Ladle into four soup plates and garnish with the warmed grapes.

HOMARD BELUGA

LOBSTER WITH CAVIAR	4 × 450 g/1 lb live Scottish hen lobsters	*Serves 4*

Cook the lobsters one at a time in the boiling vegetable stock for 5 minutes. Drain and refresh. Carefully remove the shells, keeping the tails and claws whole (page 202).

Crush the lobster shells very finely (page 201) and mix with the egg white, mirepoix and chopped tomatoes. Mix in the cold chicken stock. Add the peppercorns, a sprig of fresh thyme, salt and pepper. Bring the stock slowly to the boil, stirring frequently with a metal spoon. As soon as a froth forms on top of the stock, stop stirring, and simmer over a very gentle heat for 1 hour. Then pass through fine muslin.

Cook the vegetable diamonds in a

Ingredients
4 × 450 g/1 lb live Scottish hen lobsters
1 litre/1¾ pints vegetable stock (page 206)
1 egg white
40 g/1½ oz mirepoix (page 207)
100 g/4 oz plum tomato fillets, finely chopped
1 litre/1¾ pints strong chicken stock (page 194)
24 peppercorns, crushed
1 sprig of fresh thyme
100 g/4 oz leek diamonds
100 g/4 oz carrot diamonds
40 g/1½ oz young spinach leaves
40 g/1½ oz Beluga caviar
8 long fresh chives
salt and freshly milled pepper
10 g/¼ oz truffle julienne

small amount of lobster consommé. Blanch the spinach leaves for 10 seconds in boiling salted water. Drain and refresh, then dry on a kitchen cloth.

Overlap the spinach leaves to form eight small squares and spoon a little caviar on to each square. Fold over the leaves to form eight small, neat parcels. Tie each parcel with a fresh chive and finish with a decorative bow.

Cut the lobster tails in half and warm them very quickly with the lobster claws and knuckles in the consommé. Add the vegetable diamonds.

Pour the consommé into four soup plates. Add two caviar parcels to each portion and garnish the lobster with truffle julienne.

BROCHETTES DE LANGOUSTINE DIANA

SKEWERED LANGOUSTINES DIANA

450 g / 1 lb medium-sized courgettes
24–32 cooked langoustine tails
50 ml / 2 fl oz olive oil
50 g / 2 oz unsalted butter
200 g / 7 oz noodles (page 199)
150 ml / ¼ pint tomato coulis (page 204)
salt and freshly milled pepper

Serves 4

Peel two of the courgettes and cut the peel in long strips (discard the centres of these courgettes). Blanch the strips in boiling salted water and refresh. Cut the remaining courgettes in long, paper-thin slices. Season the courgettes with salt and pepper.

Wrap each langoustine in a slice of courgette and thread six to eight on to each skewer. Fry in the oil and half the butter until golden brown.

Toss the noodles and courgette strips in the remaining butter. Season and arrange in the centre of each plate.

Warm the tomato coulis. Position the langoustines on top of the noodles and pour some of the coulis around each portion.

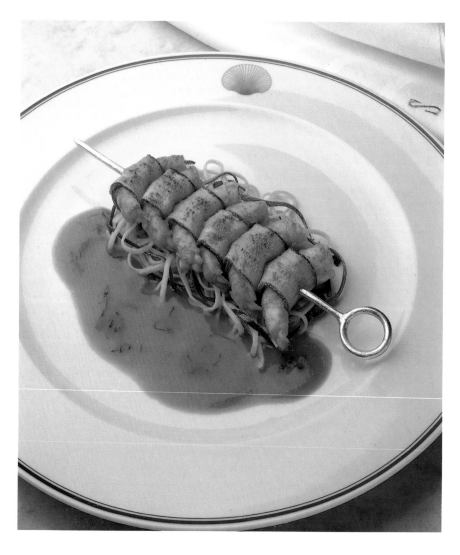

MEDAILLONS D'HOMARD D'ECOSSE AUX GINGEMBRE ET OIGNONS VERTS

LOBSTER MEDALLIONS WITH GINGER AND SPRING ONIONS

Serves 4

4 × 450 g / 1 lb live Scottish hen lobsters
1 litre / 1¾ pints vegetable stock (page 206)
30 spring onions
75 g / 3 oz unsalted butter
100 ml / 3½ fl oz Sauternes
400 ml / 14 fl oz white wine sauce (page 206)
2.5-cm / 1-inch piece of root ginger, finely grated
4 Timbales de Broccoli (page 180)
12 button onions, cooked in salted water
40 g / 1½ oz beetroot, turned and cooked in salted water
40 g / 1½ oz cucumber, turned and cooked in salted water
salt and freshly milled pepper
dried lobster eggs (page 207), optional

Cook the lobsters one at a time in the boiling vegetable stock for 5 minutes. Drain and refresh. Carefully remove the shells so that the tails and claws remain whole.

Cut four of the spring onions in fine julienne and blanch. Blanch twelve of the spring onions until tender and tie in knots. Cut the remaining spring onions in paysanne and sweat in 25 g / 1 oz of the butter in a covered saucepan for about 3 minutes until tender. Season with salt and pepper.

Reduce the Sauternes, then add the white wine sauce and ginger. Pass through fine muslin. Add the julienne of spring onions to the sauce and stir in 25 g / 1 oz of the butter. Place a little of the spring onion paysanne on each plate.

Warm the lobsters quickly in the sauce. Cut each lobster tail in medallions, then re-assemble in sequence on top of the spring onion paysanne.

Arrange the claws and knuckles around the medallions and spoon a little sauce over each portion. Unmould the timbales and position one on each plate. Warm the button onions, beetroot, cucumber and spring onion knots in the remaining butter and use to garnish each portion. Sprinkle with dried lobster eggs, if wished.

PETIT GATEAU DE CRABE BOSTON

BOSTON CRAB MOUSSE

This dish has been in The Savoy repertoire for many years. Its title acknowledges the special American connection that has existed since the hotel first opened in 1889. Shellfish is abundant along the New England coast but Bostonians may not be familiar with this method of serving crab.

Ingredients
1 live large king crab
½ egg white
300 ml / ½ pint double cream
½ egg yolk
1 litre / 1¾ pints vegetable stock (page 206)
cooked small crab claws (optional)
65 g / 2½ oz green pepper
20 g / ¾ oz red pepper
1 corn-on-the-cob
50 g / 2 oz unsalted butter
25 ml / 1 fl oz brandy
10 g / ¼ oz shallot, chopped
100 ml / 3½ fl oz dry white wine
100 ml / 3½ fl oz chicken stock (page 194)
salt and freshly milled pepper

Serves 4

Kill the crab by plunging in boiling water for 1 minute and then refresh.

Remove one large claw from the crab. Crack the shell and remove all the meat from the claw. Pass it through a fine sieve into a bowl set over ice. Keeping the bowl over the ice, add the egg white slowly, stirring constantly. Slowly beat in 100 ml / 3½ fl oz of the cream, then add the egg yolk and season the mousseline generously with salt and pepper.

Cook the crab in the boiling vegetable stock for 15 minutes. Remove and refresh.

Crack the shell and remove all the white crab meat from the remaining large claw and the small claws, taking care that no shells remain in the meat.

Add 10 g / ¼ oz of the white crab meat to the crab mousseline. Butter four 10-cm/4-inch diameter and 2-cm/¾-inch deep moulds. If wished, place a cooked crab claw in each mould. Divide the crab mousseline between the moulds and cover with clingfilm. Steam for about 6 minutes.

Reserve 25 g / 1 oz of the green pepper. Blanch the red and remaining green pepper separately in boiling salted water for 30 seconds, then drain and refresh. Peel off the skin and cut the peppers in small dice.

Blanch the corn-on-the-cob in boiling salted water for 6 minutes. Remove the kernels from the cob. Drain and refresh.

Reduce 100 ml / 3½ fl oz of the cream by half. Sweat the remaining white crab meat, all the diced green pepper, about two-thirds of the diced red pepper and the corn kernels in 25 g / 1 oz of the butter. Flame with the brandy and add the reduced cream. Season with salt and pepper.

Cut the reserved green pepper in brunoise. Sweat the shallot in 15 g / ½ oz of the butter until transparent. Add the green pepper and sweat in a covered saucepan for 2 minutes. Add the white wine and chicken stock and cook until the green pepper is tender. Add the remaining cream and simmer for a further 3–4 minutes, then purée in a liquidiser or food processor. Pass through a fine sieve, return to the heat and reduce to the required consistency. Season with salt and pepper and stir in 15 g / ½ oz of the butter.

Place a little of the creamed crab meat in the centre of each plate. Unmould a crab mousseline on top. Pour a little green pepper sauce around each portion. Toss the reserved red pepper in the remaining butter until warm and use to garnish the sauce.

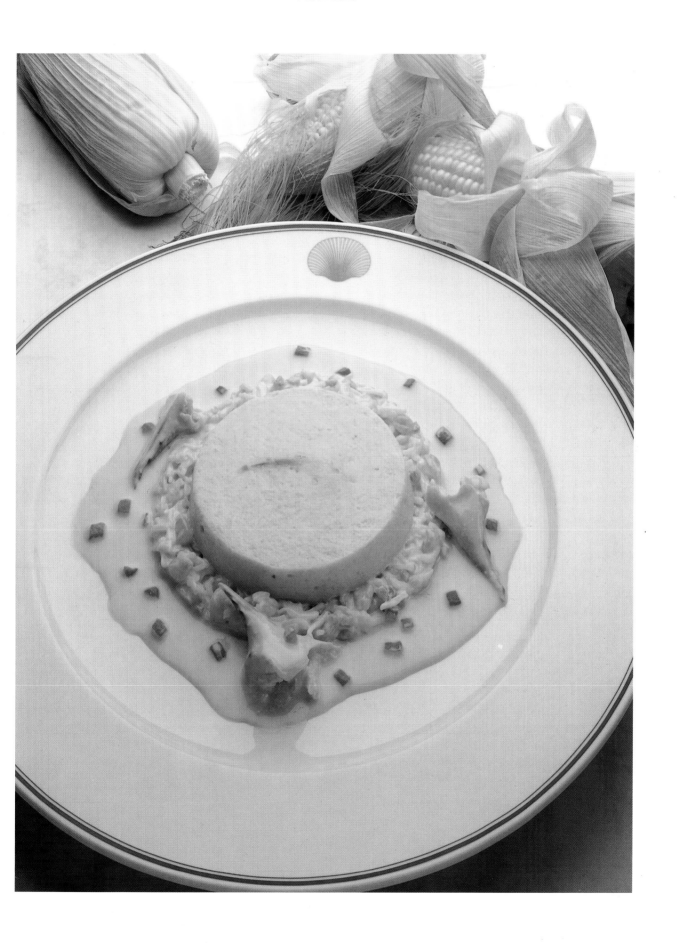

POT-POURRI DE QUENELLES DE PECHEUR

POT-POURRI OF FISH QUENELLES

Divide the fish mousse in two equal portions. Bring half the cream to the boil, add a generous pinch of saffron strands and boil until very thick. Leave to cool, then pass through muslin on to one portion of fish mousse. Mix well.

Shape four medium-sized quenelles from each portion of fish mousse. Repeat with the lobster mousse. Poach all the quenelles in the well seasoned vegetable stock for about 6 minutes, making sure that the stock never boils after it has been poured on to the fish quenelles.

Sweat half the shallot in 25 g/1 oz of the butter. Add the watercress, sweat, then add the white wine and reduce. Add half the white wine sauce and simmer for about 1 minute, then liquidise. Pass through a fine sieve or muslin. Reduce to the required consistency, season to taste and stir in 15 g/½ oz of the butter.

350 g/12 oz fish mousse (page 196)
100 ml/3½ fl oz double cream
saffron strands
175 g/6 oz lobster mousse (page 197)
500 ml/18 fl oz vegetable stock (page 206)
10 g/¼ oz shallot, chopped
75 g/3 oz unsalted butter
100 g/4 oz watercress, roughly chopped
50 ml/2 fl oz dry white wine
300 ml/½ pint white wine sauce (page 206)
50 ml/2 fl oz Noilly Prat
40 g/1½ oz chanterelles, cleaned
25 ml/1 fl oz olive oil
100 g/4 oz young spinach leaves
salt and freshly milled pepper
100 ml/3½ fl oz lobster sauce (page 198)
4 fleurons (page 196)

Serves 4

Place the Noilly Prat and a pinch of saffron in a saucepan and warm to dissolve. Add the remaining white wine sauce and simmer for about 1 minute. Pass through a fine sieve or muslin. Reduce to the required consistency, season to taste and stir in 15 g/½ oz of the butter.

Sweat the remaining shallot in the remaining butter until transparent. Add the chanterelles and sweat for about 1 minute. Season to taste.

Heat the oil and toss the spinach leaves very quickly. Season with salt and pepper and arrange a few on each plate. Arrange three quenelles beside each portion of spinach. Spoon a little lobster sauce over each saffron quenelle, a little saffron sauce over each fish mousse quenelle and a little watercress sauce over each lobster quenelle. Garnish with chanterelles and fleurons.

LES VIANDES,
LES VOLAILLES ET
LE GIBIER

PAUPIETTES DE VEAU VITTORIO

VEAL VITTORIO

This dish has recently been named after Vittorio, who is the butcher in The Savoy kitchens. He shares the record for long service with Maurice, for whom Perdreau braisé aux marrons Maurice *has been named.*

Cut the fillet of veal in eight equal portions and flatten each piece between sheets of plastic.

Sweat half the chopped onion in 15 g/½ oz of the butter and half the oil until transparent. Leave to cool.

Add the sautéed onion, a sprinkling of herbs, the egg, half the cream and the Gruyère to the minced veal. Mix well and season with salt and pepper.

Spread a little of the mixture over each piece of veal. Fold in the sides and roll each piece neatly to make a paupiette. Wrap two pieces of bacon around each paupiette and secure with wooden cocktail sticks.

Heat the remaining oil and

400 g/14 oz fillet of veal
40 g/1½ oz onion, chopped
90 g/3½ oz unsalted butter
25 ml/1 fl oz olive oil
freshly chopped herbs such as tarragon, parsley or chives
1 egg, beaten
100 ml/3½ fl oz double cream
20 g/¾ oz Gruyère, finely chopped
100 g/4 oz veal, finely minced
8 rashers of streaky bacon, cut in half
10 g/¼ oz shallot, chopped
100 g/4 oz button mushrooms
100 ml/3½ fl oz dry sherry
200 ml/7 fl oz jus de veau (page 197)
1 clove of garlic, crushed
750 g/1 lb 12 oz plum tomato fillets, chopped
½ bay leaf
4 portions of Gnocchi alla Romana (page 186)
salt and freshly milled pepper
20 tiny sage leaves

Serves 4

25 g/1 oz of the butter in a sauteuse. Season the paupiettes with salt and pepper, brown on all sides, then cook at 180°C/350°F/gas mark 4 for about 10 minutes until golden brown. Remove from the sauteuse and keep warm. Discard the fat.

Sweat the shallot in 25 g/1 oz of the butter. Add to the mushrooms and sweat for a further 1 minute. Add the sherry and reduce by half. Add the jus de veau and remaining cream and reduce to the required consistency. Season to taste and stir in 15 g/½ oz of the butter.

Sweat the remaining onion and garlic in the remaining butter. Add the tomato, bay leaf, salt and pepper. Simmer for about 10 minutes.

Arrange two paupiettes on each plate, and spoon a little sauce over each portion. Spoon a little tomato on each plate, top with a portion of Gnocchi alla Romana and garnish with sage leaves.

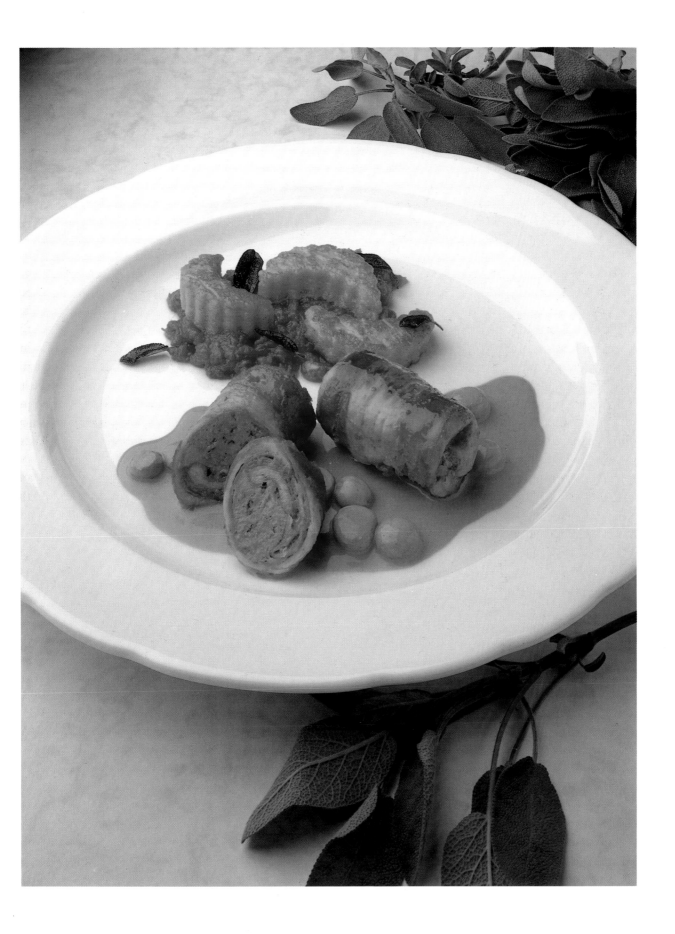

CANON D'AGNEAU POCHE, SAUCE RAIFORT

POACHED LAMB WITH HORSERADISH SAUCE

2 racks of lamb
40 g / 1½ oz carrot, cut in brunoise
40 g / 1½ oz leek, cut in brunoise
40 g / 1½ oz celery, cut in brunoise
50 g / 2 oz unsalted butter
400 g / 14 oz new potatoes, cut in 5-mm / ¼-inch cubes
1 litre / 1¾ pints strong chicken stock (page 194)
50 ml / 2 fl oz dry white wine
200 ml / 7 fl oz double cream
freshly grated horseradish
10 g / ¼ oz freshly chopped parsley
salt and freshly milled pepper

Serves 4

Remove all the bones and fat from the racks of lamb.

Sweat the diced vegetables quickly in 25 g / 1 oz of the butter.

Place the potatoes in a saucepan of cold salted water and quickly bring to the boil. Drain and add to the diced vegetables. Add about half of the stock, to just cover. Season with salt and pepper. Simmer gently for about 10 minutes until tender.

Bring the remaining chicken stock to the boil, reduce to a simmer and add the lamb. Poach gently without boiling for 8 minutes until the lamb is pink.

Remove the lamb from the saucepan and keep warm.

Reduce the white wine, then add the chicken stock and reduce. Add the cream, freshly grated horseradish to taste and freshly chopped parsely. Season to taste and stir in the remaining butter.

Cut the lamb in 5-mm / ¼-inch thick slices and arrange some on each plate. Position some potatoes on each plate and pour a small amount of stock over the meat. Serve the horseradish sauce separately and pour on to the meat at the last minute.

TOURNEDOS
DE BOEUF BACCHUS

TOURNEDOS WITH WILD MUSHROOMS

Heat the oil and 25 g/1 oz of the butter and fry the tournedos quickly on both sides to seal, then cook according to personal taste. Remove from the pan and keep warm.

Discard the fat, add 15 g/½ oz of the butter and half the shallot. Sweat until transparent, then add the snails and red wine, and reduce. Add the jus de veau and reduce to the required consistency. Season to taste and stir in 15 g/½ oz of the butter.

Ingredients
50 ml/2 fl oz oil
75 g/3 oz unsalted butter
4 × 165 g/5½ oz tournedos of beef
20 g/¾ oz shallot, chopped
65 g/2½ oz prepared snails, cut in quarters
100 ml/3½ fl oz red wine
200 ml/7 fl oz jus de veau (page 197)
100 g/4 oz assorted wild mushrooms, cleaned
freshly chopped herbs such as tarragon and chervil
4 Pommes Savoyard (page 180)
salt and freshly milled pepper

Serves 4

Place the remaining shallot and the remaining butter in a saucepan and sweat. Add the wild mushrooms and sweat for about 2 minutes. Season to taste and add the herbs.

Place a Pomme Savoyard on each plate and position a tournedos on each one. Pour a little sauce over each portion and garnish with the wild mushrooms.

Serve with Légumes Variés Royal (page 188).

COTE DE VEAU NORMANDE

VEAL CUTLET NORMANDE

Melt 50 g/2 oz of the butter and fry the veal cutlets until just pink. Remove from the pan and discard the fat. Sweat the onions in 15 g/½ oz of the butter until transparent. Add the peppercorns and cider and reduce by two-thirds. Add the jus de veau and cream, and reduce to the desired consistency. Season with salt and pepper and pass through fine muslin.

Sweat the mushrooms in 15 g/½ oz of the butter. Add the sauce to the mushrooms and stir in 15 g/½ oz of the butter and a sprinkling of herbs.

100 g/4 oz unsalted butter
4 × 250 g/9 oz veal cutlets, all fat removed
40 g/1½ oz onion, finely chopped
24 white peppercorns, crushed
300 ml/½ pint dry cider
200 ml/7 fl oz jus de veau (page 197)
100 ml/3½ fl oz double cream
65 g/2½ oz button mushrooms
freshly chopped herbs
50 g/2 oz puff paste (page 200)
1 dessert apple, quartered, peeled and cored
1 egg yolk, beaten
poppy seeds
sesame seeds
400 g/14 oz spinach leaves, blanched
ground nutmeg
salt and freshly milled pepper

Serves 4

Roll out the puff paste and use to wrap each apple quarter. Brush with beaten egg yolk and cover with a sprinkling of poppy and sesame seeds. Leave to rest for 20 minutes, then bake at 200°C/400°F/gas mark 6 for about 15 minutes until golden brown.

Thoroughly dry the spinach and toss very quickly in the remaining butter. Season with nutmeg, salt and pepper.

Place some spinach on each plate, arrange a veal cutlet on the top, spoon some sauce and mushrooms over and garnish with an apple fleuron.

ROSETTES DE BOEUF AU CERFEUIL

ROSETTES OF BEEF WITH CHERVIL

100 g / 4 oz small young carrots
sugar
65 g / 2½ oz unsalted butter
100 g / 4 oz very small courgettes
200 g / 7 oz Cannoise (page 193)
550 g / 1¼ lb fillet of beef, cut in 8 rosettes
50 ml / 2 fl oz dry white wine
100 ml / 3½ fl oz jus de veau (page 197)
100 ml / 3½ fl oz double cream
20 g / ¾ oz Meaux mustard
salt and freshly milled pepper
20 sprigs of chervil

Serves 4

Canalé the carrots and cut in 3-mm/ ⅛-inch thick slices. Place a generous pinch of sugar and 10 g / ¼ oz of the butter in a saucepan and add a small amount of water. Cover and cook the carrots until tender.

Peel two of the courgettes, blanch the peel in boiling salted water, drain and refresh. Canalé the remaining courgettes, then blanch in boiling salted water. Refresh and cut in 3-mm / ⅛-inch thick slices. Melt 15 g / ½ oz of the butter and toss the courgette slices very quickly. Season with salt and pepper.

Warm the Cannoise. Place a 9–10-cm / 3½–4-inch metal ring on each plate. Half-fill with Cannoise and level the surface. Remove the rings. Arrange the sliced carrots and sliced courgettes decoratively on the top. Warm the courgette skins and wrap around the Cannoise chartreuse.

Heat 25 g / 1 oz of the butter and fry the rosettes of beef on both sides according to taste. Remove from the pan and discard the fat. Déglacé with the white wine, reduce and add the jus de veau and cream. Reduce to the desired consistency. Stir in the mustard, season to taste and stir in the remaining butter.

Pour a little sauce on each plate, arrange the rosettes of beef on top and garnish with sprigs of chervil.

ESCALOPES DE ROGNONS ET RIS DE VEAU AUX OIGNONS VERTS

KIDNEY AND SWEETBREAD WITH HORSE-RADISH AND SPRING ONION SAUCE

Ingredients	
350 g / 12 oz veal sweetbread, prepared	
350 g / 12 oz veal kidneys	
75 g / 3 oz unsalted butter	
sugar	
100 g / 4 oz young carrots	
8 spring onions	
100 g / 4 oz asparagus tips	
plain flour	
50 ml / 2 fl oz oil	
50 ml / 2 fl oz dry white wine	
50 ml / 2 fl oz chicken stock (page 194)	
50 ml / 2 fl oz vegetable stock (page 206)	
100 ml / 3½ fl oz double cream	
20 g / ¾ oz freshly grated horseradish	
freshly chopped parsley	
salt and freshly milled pepper	

Serves 4

Cut the veal sweetbread in 1-cm/½-inch thick slices. Cut the veal kidneys in 1-cm/½-inch thick slices, leaving a very small amount of fat around each slice.

Place a small knob of butter and a generous pinch of sugar in a saucepan and caramelise lightly. Add the carrots and toss in this glaze. Add 25 ml/1 fl oz of water or vegetable stock, salt and pepper, cover and cook until al dente.

Cook four of the spring onions in boiling salted water until al dente and refresh. Cook the asparagus tips in boiling salted water until al dente and refresh. Cut the remaining spring onions in very small dice.

Season the veal kidneys and veal sweetbread with salt and pepper, then dust lightly with flour. Heat the oil and 25 g/1 oz of the butter. Fry the kidneys until pink and fry the sweetbread very quickly on both sides until golden brown. Remove from the pan and keep warm.

Discard the fat from the pan, add 10 g/¼ oz of the butter and sweat the finely chopped spring onions. Add the white wine, chicken and vegetable stocks and reduce. Add the cream and reduce to the required consistency. Add the freshly grated horseradish to the sauce, season to taste and stir in 25 g/1 oz of the butter. Stir in a little chopped parsley.

Melt the remaining butter and toss all the vegetables. Season with salt and pepper. Spoon a little sauce on to each plate.

Arrange the sweetbread and kidneys alternately on the sauce. Garnish with the vegetables.

LES TROIS ROSETTES
SUR SPAGHETTI DE LEGUMES AU SAUCE DE CORIANDRE

ROSETTES OF VEAL, BEEF AND LAMB

Cut all the carrots and kohlrabi in 'spaghetti', but only cut the outside skin of the courgettes in 'spaghetti'. Blanch in boiling salted water for about 1 minute, then refresh.

Cut the potatoes in cylindrical shapes, about 4-cm/1½-inch diameter, then cut in wafer-thin slices. Dry on a kitchen cloth and toss in hot oil until just tender but not coloured. Drain and dry. Season with salt and pepper.

Reserve about 10 g/¼ oz of the fresh coriander for the sauce. Place one large coriander leaf on a slice of potato and cover with another slice of potato. Press down well. Repeat until all the slices of potato and coriander leaves are used.

Heat the oil and 25 g/1 oz of the

Ingredients
100 g/4 oz carrots
100 g/4 oz kohlrabi
100 g/4 oz courgettes
500 g/1 lb 2 oz potatoes
oil for blanching
40 g/1½ oz fresh coriander
50 ml/2 fl oz oil
175 g/6 oz unsalted butter
200 g/7 oz fillet of veal, trimmed and cut in 4 rosettes
200 g/7 oz fillet of beef, trimmed and cut in 4 rosettes
200 g/7 oz loin of lamb, trimmed and cut in 4 rosettes
100 ml/3½ fl oz Noilly Prat
50 ml/2 fl oz jus de veau (page 197)
200 ml/7 fl oz double cream
salt and freshly milled pepper

Serves 4

butter and fry the rosettes of meat on both sides according to taste. Remove from the pan and keep warm.

Discard the fat from the pan and déglacé with the Noilly Prat. Add the jus de veau and cream, and reduce to the required consistency.

Chop the reserved coriander, add to the sauce, season with salt and pepper and stir in 15 g/½ oz of the butter.

Melt 40 g/1½ oz of the butter and toss the vegetable 'spaghetti' until warm. Season and arrange some in the middle of each plate. Place the rosettes of meat on top.

Fry the slices of potato very quickly in the remaining butter until they are crisp and golden, then drain on a kitchen cloth. Arrange around the meat and pour some sauce over each portion.

FOIE DE VEAU
AU CONFIT D'ECHALOTES ET MIEL

CALF'S LIVER WITH SHALLOTS

600 g / 1¼ lb calf's liver
20 g / ¾ oz plain flour
50 ml / 2 fl oz oil
100 g / 4 oz unsalted butter
200 ml / 7 fl oz dry white wine
300 ml / ½ pint jus de veau (page 197)
25 g / 1 oz plum tomato diamonds
fresh thyme leaves
200 g / 7 oz shallots, finely chopped
½ clove of garlic, crushed
50 ml / 2 fl oz herb-flavoured white wine vinegar
15 g / ½ oz honey
20 g / ¾ oz fresh herbs such as chervil, basil and chives
salt and freshly milled pepper

Serves 4

Peel the skin from the calf's liver and cut in thin slices. Season with salt and pepper and dust with the flour. Heat the oil and half the butter and fry the liver very quickly on both sides so it remains pink. Remove from the pan and keep warm.

Discard the fat remaining in the pan, déglacé with half the white wine and reduce. Add the jus de veau, season to taste and stir in half the remaining butter, the tomato diamonds and a sprinkling of fresh thyme leaves.

Sweat the shallots and garlic in the remaining butter until transparent and very soft. Add the vinegar and reduce. Add the remaining white wine and reduce. Add the honey and herbs, and season to taste.

Arrange a little of the shallot mixture in the centre of each plate, place slices of calf's liver on top and pour the sauce around each portion.

MIGNONS DE VEAU AUX CEPES

MIGNONS OF VEAL WITH CEPS

100 g/4 oz unsalted butter
50 ml/2 fl oz oil
8 × 75 g/3 oz mignons of veal
10 g/¼ oz shallot, chopped
½ clove of garlic, crushed
100 g/4 oz fresh ceps, cleaned and sliced
100 ml/3½ fl oz dry white wine
200 ml/7 fl oz jus de veau (page 197)
100 g/4 oz assorted noodles (page 199)
freshly chopped mixed herbs such as chervil, chives and tarragon
salt and freshly milled pepper

Serves 4

Heat 25 g/1 oz of the butter and the oil, and fry the mignons of veal until pink. Remove from the pan and keep in a warm place. Discard the fat.

Sweat half the shallots in 25 g/1 oz of the butter until transparent. Add the garlic and sweat for a further minute. Add the ceps to the shallots and sweat for about 2 minutes. Season with salt and pepper and remove from the pan.

Add the remaining shallots to the pan and sweat with 15 g/½ oz of the butter. Add the white wine and reduce by two-thirds. Add the jus de veau and reduce to the required consistency. Season to taste and stir in 15 g/½ oz of the butter.

Cook the noodles in a large amount of boiling salted water with a dash of oil until al dente. Refresh, then drain and toss in the remaining butter. Season to taste.

Twist about a quarter of the noodles on a fork into a spiral on each plate, arrange the mignons on top, spoon a little sauce over each and garnish with ceps, sprinkled with herbs.

NOISETTES D'AGNEAU NICOISES

NOISETTES OF LAMB NICOISE

Canalé the courgettes evenly, then blanch in boiling salted water for about 2 minutes. Drain and refresh, then cut at an angle in slices about 3-mm/⅛-inch thick.

Dry the courgette flowers on a kitchen cloth and cut the courgettes in thin slices to fan out. Remove the stamens from inside the flowers and fill with the Cannoise. Place in a buttered dish, season and cover with clingfilm. Steam for about 3 minutes.

Heat the oil and 25 g/1 oz of the butter, and fry the noisettes until pink, turning frequently. Remove from the pan and discard the fat. Add the Madeira and truffle juice, and reduce by half. Add the jus de veau and reduce to the required consistency. Pass through a fine sieve or muslin. Season to taste,

Ingredients
2 small green courgettes
2 small yellow courgettes
4 tiny courgettes with their flowers, blanched
65 g/2½ oz Cannoise (page 193)
50 ml/2 fl oz oil
100 g/4 oz unsalted butter
8 × 75 g/3 oz noisettes of lamb (page 193)
25 ml/1 fl oz Madeira
50 ml/2 fl oz truffle juice (page 198)
300 ml/½ pint jus de veau (page 197)
10 g/¼ oz truffle, chopped
150 g/5 oz mushroom duxelle (page 199)
1 clove of garlic, crushed
1 plum tomato, cut in fillets
20 g/¾ oz fresh foie gras, cut in 4 small rounds
plain flour
4 slices of truffle
salt and freshly milled pepper

Serves 4

stir in 25 g/1 oz of the butter and add the chopped truffle.

Arrange some hot mushroom duxelle in a neat circle on each plate.

Melt 25 g/1 oz of the butter with the crushed garlic and toss the courgette slices and tomato fillets until warm. Season to taste and arrange around the mushroom duxelle.

Place two noisettes on each plate.

Season the foie gras and dust with flour. Fry very quickly on both sides in the remaining butter in a heavy-based pan. Warm the slices of truffle in the sauce.

Spoon a little sauce over the noisettes. Place the foie gras on top and garnish with the slices of truffle. Fan a filled courgette flower carefully on each plate.

CANETON SOUFFLE AU CHATELAIN DE TOURBILLON

THE SQUIRE OF TOURBILLON'S DUCK

Featured regularly on the Restaurant menu now, this dish exemplifies the spirit of freemasonry that exists between distinguished chefs. It was created by Virlogeux, maître-chef of the Grill in the glittering years between the wars. He subsequently moved to another hotel where he gave the recipe to a young colleague, who in turn passed it back to Anton Edelmann many years later!

Bone out the duck with a small knife (page 205). Reserve all the bones.

Sweat the shallots and garlic in the oil and 25 g/1 oz of the butter until transparent. Add the mushrooms and sweat for 1–2 minutes. Add half the truffle juice. Reduce, then leave to cool. Add to the boned duck meat and pork, and mince coarsely.

Finely mince the pork fat with the breadcrumbs and add to the meat mixture. Combine with the egg, egg yolk, double cream, chopped truffle and diced foie gras, and season generously. Use this mixture to fill the duck and

Ingredients
1 duck, dressed
40 g/1½ oz shallots, finely chopped
½ clove of garlic, crushed
50 ml/2 fl oz oil
65 g/2½ oz unsalted butter
100 g/4 oz mushrooms, cut in quarters
100 ml/3½ fl oz truffle juice (page 198)
100 g/4 oz boned duck thigh meat
200 g/7 oz loin of pork
50 g/2 oz pork fat
50 g/2 oz fresh white breadcrumbs, soaked in a little milk and squeezed
1 egg
1 egg yolk
50 ml/2 fl oz double cream
10 g/¼ oz truffle, chopped
25 g/1 oz foie gras, diced
100 g/4 oz mirepoix (page 207)
2 large duck breasts
50 ml/2 fl oz ruby port
300 ml/½ pint jus de veau (page 197)
75 g/3 oz grapes, peeled and pips removed
50 g/2 oz walnut halves, blanched in milk and peeled
salt and freshly milled pepper
12–16 sprigs of chervil

Serves 6–8

reshape. Sew up all the openings with a trussing needle and fine string.

Melt half the remaining butter, brush the duck and season generously. Place in a roasting tin on the duck bones and mirepoix and roast at 180°C/350°F/gas mark 4 for about 1 hour, basting frequently. Add the duck breasts to the roasting tin and cook for a further 15 minutes. Remove from the oven and leave to rest in a warm place for at least 15 minutes.

Discard the fat from the roasting tin. Add the remaining truffle juice, port and jus de veau. Simmer for 15 minutes, skimming frequently. Season with salt and pepper and stir in the remaining butter. Pass through a fine sieve or muslin.

Cut the duck in 1-cm/½-inch thick slices and place one in the centre of each plate. Remove the skin from the duck breasts, cut in thin slices and arrange a few on each plate. Add the grapes and walnuts to the sauce and pour a little around each portion. Garnish with sprigs of chervil.

DELICE DE VOLAILLE
A LA HOMARDINE

CHICKEN SUPREME WITH LOBSTER FILLING

Remove the fillet from each chicken suprême and split by making a cut horizontally almost through each one. Open out and place all the pieces of chicken between sheets of plastic and beat lightly to flatten (page 192). Season with salt and pepper.

Pass the raw lobster eggs through a fine sieve, add to the chicken mousse and mix well. Spread a little chicken mousse very thinly on each suprême, leaving a 5-mm/¼-inch border. Dry the spinach, season and lay on top of the chicken mousse. Spread another thin layer of chicken mousse on top.

Place half a lobster tail on each suprême and top with the reserved chicken fillet. Fold the pointed end and sides of the chicken breast over the

Ingredients
4 × 120 g/4½ oz chicken suprêmes, trimmed
10 g/¼ oz raw lobster eggs
75 g/3 oz chicken mousse (page 206)
65 g/2½ oz young spinach leaves, blanched
2 × 450 g/1 lb Scottish hen lobsters, cooked for 5 minutes (page 207), shells removed
65 g/2½ oz unsalted butter
150 g/5 oz vegetables such as carrots, courgettes, turnips and swede, cut in batons and blanched
200 ml/7 fl oz lobster sauce (page 198)
40 g/1½ oz wild rice, cooked
65 g/2½ oz pilaff rice (page 200)
65 g/2½ oz saffron rice (page 200)
10 g/¼ oz freshly chopped herbs such as chervil, tarragon and coriander
salt and freshly milled pepper
dried lobster eggs (page 207), optional

Serves 4

lobster to form a neat parcel. Wrap each piece of chicken in clingfilm and steam for about 8 minutes.

Melt 40 g/1½ oz of the butter and sauté the vegetable batons, season to taste and arrange some on each plate.

Remove the clingfilm from the chicken breasts, cut in slices and arrange on top of the vegetables. Warm the lobster claws and arrange on one side of the chicken. Pour a little sauce around each portion.

Mix the three rices with the herbs. Melt the remaining butter and toss the rice mixture until warm. Season to taste and arrange a little on each plate. Sprinkle each portion with dried lobster eggs, if wished.

POULET SAUTE
A LA ROMAINE

ROMAN-STYLE CHICKEN SAUTE	2 × 1.25/kg/2½ lb chickens, dressed	*Serves 4*
	10 g/¼ oz plain flour	
	50 ml/2 fl oz oil	
	75 g/3 oz unsalted butter	
	50 g/2 oz onion, finely chopped	
	½ clove of garlic, crushed	
	100 g/4 oz plum tomato fillets, chopped	
	120 g/4½ oz button mushrooms, cut in quarters	
	1 red pepper, cut in small triangles	
	1 green pepper, cut in small triangles	
	100 ml/3½ fl oz dry white wine	
	300 ml/½ pint jus de veau (page 197)	
	1 sprig of sage, chopped	
	1 sprig of rosemary, chopped	
	salt and freshly milled pepper	
	200 g/7 oz Polenta (page 186), cut in diamonds	

Remove the legs and winglets from each chicken. Cut the chickens in half. Cut off the knuckle from each chicken drumstick and scrape the tip of the bone clean. Remove the thigh bone from each thigh. Make an incision in the centre of each thigh and push the drumstick bone through the cut to form a neat shape (page 206). Trim each breast. Season all the pieces of chicken with salt and pepper, and dust with the flour.

Heat half the oil and 25 g/1 oz of the butter and fry the chicken until golden brown on all sides. Remove from the pan and discard the fat.

Add the remaining oil and 25 g/1 oz of the butter to the pan and sweat the onion slowly until transparent. Add the garlic, tomato and mushrooms and sweat for a further 2 minutes. Add the peppers and wine, and reduce. Add the jus de veau, sage and rosemary.

Return the pieces of chicken to the pan, season with salt and pepper, cover and braise at 180°C/350°F/gas mark 4 for about 20 minutes.

Remove the chicken and remove all the bones from each breast. Reduce the sauce to the required consistency. Season to taste and stir in the remaining butter.

Arrange some of the chicken in the centre of each plate, spoon a little of the sauce on top and garnish with fried diamonds of Polenta.

SUPREME DE CANARD AUX RAISINS

DUCK SUPREME WITH GRAPES IN A PUFF PASTRY LATTICE

2 × 2 kg/4½ lb ducks, dressed
40 g/1½ oz chicken mousse (page 206)
40 g/1½ oz fresh foie gras
50 g/2 oz unsalted butter
50 ml/2 fl oz oil
50 g/2 oz mirepoix (page 207)
100 ml/3½ fl oz dry white wine
500 ml/18 fl oz jus de veau (page 197)
120 g/4½ oz puff paste (page 200)
1 egg yolk, beaten
65 g/2½ oz green lentils, soaked in cold water for at least 4 hours
65 g/2½ oz vegetables such as leek, celery and carrot, cut in brunoise
100 g/4 oz carrot purée (page 193)
100 g/4 oz celeriac purée (page 193)
12 turned carrots (page 181), cooked in stock
12 turned turnips (page 181), cooked in stock
40 g/1½ oz mangetout, blanched
100 g/4 oz white grapes, peeled and pips removed
salt and freshly milled pepper
4 sprigs of chervil

Serves 4

Remove the wish-bone and legs from each duck and take off the breasts. Remove all the fat from the breasts, then make an incision with a long, narrow-bladed knife through the centre of each breast, starting at the thick end and working right down to the pointed end to form a pocket. Fill each pocket with a small amount of chicken mousse. Cut the foie gras in batons and insert one in each breast.

Heat 15 g/½ oz of the butter and half the oil. Season the duck breasts with salt and pepper and seal very quickly on both sides. Leave to cool.

Chop the duck carcasses and legs and place in a roasting tin with the remaining oil. Cook at 220°C/425°F/ gas mark 7 for about 20 minutes or until brown.

Add the mirepoix and cook for a further 10 minutes. Discard the fat, add the white wine and reduce. Add the jus de veau and simmer for about 20 minutes, skimming frequently. Remove the bones, then pass the sauce through a fine sieve, season to taste and stir in half the remaining butter.

Roll out the puff paste about 3-mm/ ⅛-inch thick and mark with a lattice roller (page 200). Cut in four equal portions. Wrap each duck breast in a piece of lattice paste and brush with beaten egg yolk. Leave to rest for at least 20 minutes in a cool place.

Cook the lentils in boiling salted water for about 15 minutes. Drain thoroughly. Sweat the finely diced vegetables in the remaining butter until tender. Mix in the lentils and season with salt and pepper.

Bake the duck breasts at 220°C/ 425°F/gas mark 7 for 8 minutes or until golden.

Warm the carrot and celeriac purées separately. Shape four quenelles with the carrot purée, place one on each plate; shape four quenelles with the celeriac purée, place one on each plate. Arrange some of the turned carrots, turnips and mangetout on each plate. Place a little of the lentil mixture on each plate. Cut the duck breasts and arrange on top.

Add the grapes to the sauce, warm gently and pour some sauce around each duck breast. Garnish with the grapes and sprigs of chervil.

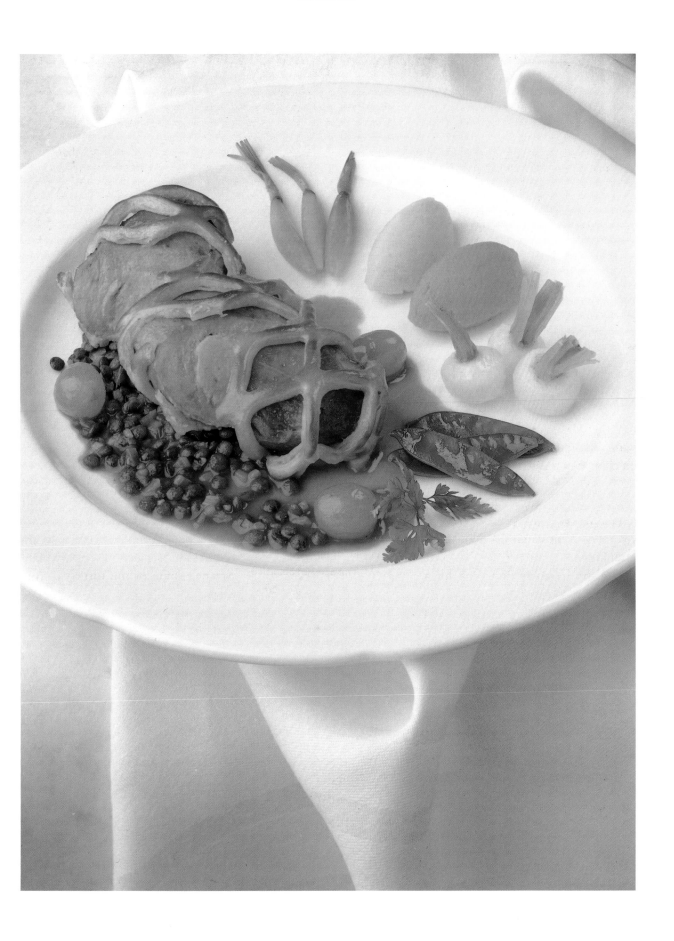

JAMBONETTE DE VOLAILLE FARCIE AUX ECREVISSES

STUFFED CHICKEN LEG WITH CRAYFISH

Serves 4

Ingredients
4 medium-sized chicken legs
10 g / ¼ oz shallot, chopped
65 g / 2½ oz unsalted butter
250 g / 9 oz button mushrooms, very finely chopped
10 g / ¼ oz freshly chopped herbs such as thyme, tarragon and chives
40 g / 1½ oz chicken mousse (page 206)
24 live crayfish
1 litre / 1¾ pints vegetable stock (page 206)
25 ml / 1 fl oz olive oil
40 g / 1½ oz mirepoix (page 207)
½ clove of garlic
50 ml / 2 fl oz brandy
20 g / ¾ oz tomato purée
100 ml / 3½ fl oz dry sherry
500 ml / 18 fl oz chicken stock (page 194)
200 ml / 7 fl oz double cream
salt and freshly milled pepper
4 sprigs of chervil

Bone out each chicken leg by easing the flesh away from the bone starting at the thigh and working down to the drumstick, taking care not to pierce the skin.

Sweat the shallot in 40 g / 1½ oz of the butter until transparent. Add the mushrooms and cook very quickly. Season with salt and pepper and leave to cool.

Add the mushrooms and herbs to the chicken mousse and mix well.

Cook the crayfish in the boiling vegetable stock for 2 minutes. Drain and refresh. Remove and reserve the shells. Trim the crayfish and reserve twenty tails for garnish. Cut the remaining tails in half and mix with the trimmings into the prepared stuffing. Season generously and use to fill the chicken legs and sew up with a trussing needle and fine string.

Season the chicken legs with salt and pepper and roast at 190°C / 375°F / gas mark 5 in 15 g / ½ oz of the butter and half the oil until golden brown and well cooked. Remove and keep warm. Discard the fat.

Chop the crayfish heads and shells very finely. Heat the remaining oil and fry the shells very quickly. Add the mirepoix and garlic, fry quickly and flame with the brandy. Add the tomato purée, half the sherry and the chicken stock, and simmer for about 20 minutes, skimming frequently. Pass through a fine sieve or muslin and reduce. Add the cream and reduce to the required consistency. Stir in the remaining sherry and butter. Season to taste.

Arrange a piece of chicken on each plate. Add the reserved crayfish to the sauce and heat gently. Spoon a little sauce over each portion.

Garnish with sprigs of chervil and serve with Crêpes aux Maïs et Poivrons (page 182).

GAME PIE

Improbable as it may sound, this popular dish was developed during the Second World War. Game was not rationed and the owners of many Scottish estates sold birds and venison to The Savoy. Obviously some of the other ingredients had to be omitted at that time. The addition of oxtail is an innovation that gives more strength to the sauce than the traditional drumstick.

Cut the game birds in half. Cut the venison in two large chunks. Season the meats with salt and pepper and dust lightly with the flour.

Heat half the oil and 25 g/1 oz of the butter and fry all the meats until golden brown. Remove from the pan and discard the fat. Add the remaining oil and 15 g/½ oz of the butter, then add the mirepoix and fry for about 5 minutes until lightly coloured. Add the garlic and tomato purée and sweat for a further 2–3 minutes, stirring constantly. Add the red wine and reduce.

Add the jus de veau, herbs and peppercorns with the oxtail and tomato. Cover with a lid and braise at 170°C/325°F/gas mark 3 for about 1½ hours. Stir occasionally, adding a little extra stock if necessary. Add the game birds and venison and braise for a further 20 minutes, or until the meats are tender. Remove from the oven and remove all the meats from the sauce.

Pass the sauce through a fine sieve or muslin, season to taste and stir in 15 g/½ oz of the butter.

Place the oxtail in a pie dish.

Ingredients
1 grouse or pheasant, dressed
1 partridge, dressed
200 g/7 oz loin or haunch of venison
20 g/¾ oz plain flour
50 ml/2 fl oz oil
75 g/3 oz unsalted butter
50 g/2 oz mirepoix (page 207)
1 clove of garlic, crushed
20 g/¾ oz tomato purée
200 ml/7 fl oz red wine
300 ml/½ pint jus de veau (page 197)
½ bay leaf
1 sprig of thyme
24 peppercorns, crushed
300 g/10 oz oxtail, cut in small pieces
20 g/¾ oz plum tomato fillets, chopped
200 g/7 oz chestnuts
10 g/¼ oz sugar
100 ml/3½ fl oz dry white wine
50 g/2 oz small button mushrooms
50 g/2 oz dried apricots, soaked in cold water for at least 1 hour
50 g/2 oz button onions, blanched
50 g/2 oz streaky bacon, cut in lardons and blanched
150 g/5 oz puff paste (page 200)
1 egg yolk, beaten
salt and freshly milled pepper

Serves 4

Remove all the bones from the game birds and divide the breast and legs. Add the venison and game birds to the pie dish.

Make a cross-shaped incision with a small knife in each chestnut and place on a baking tray and roast at 230°C/450°F/gas mark 8 until the points of the cut curl up. Remove the skin.

Place 10 g/¼ oz of the butter in a saucepan with the sugar and lightly caramelise. Add the white wine and reduce. Add the chestnuts and stir well until glazed. Reduce all the cooking liquid, add a small amount of the sauce and reduce until the chestnuts are evenly coated.

Melt the remaining butter and sauté the mushrooms very quickly. Season with salt and pepper. Add the apricots, chestnuts, button onions, bacon lardons and mushrooms to the sauce and pour the sauce on to the meats.

Roll out the puff paste thinly to about 2.5-cm/1-inch larger in diameter than the pie dish. Brush the edges of the paste with egg yolk and place egg-side down over the pie dish so that it overhangs. Garnish with the trimmings and criss-cross the surface with the back of a knife. Leave to rest for 20 minutes in a cool place, then brush with egg yolk. Bake at 200°C/400°F/gas mark 6 for about 25 minutes until golden brown. Trim the excess pastry from around the pie dish.

Serve with Navets à la Dauphinoise (page 182).

CAILLE FARCIE
A LA DAUPHINOISE

**STUFFED QUAIL WITH
DAUPHINE POTATOES**

4 quails, dressed
75 g/3 oz stuffing for quail (page 201)
50 ml/2 fl oz oil
40 g/1½ oz mirepoix (page 207)
200 ml/7 fl oz dry white wine
300 ml/½ pint jus de veau (page 197)
12 peppercorns, crushed
65 g/2½ oz unsalted butter
1 clove of garlic, halved
500 g/1 lb 2 oz new potatoes, cut in 3-mm/⅛-inch slices
ground nutmeg
50 g/2 oz Gruyère, grated
300 ml/½ pint double cream
10 g/¼ oz caster sugar
75 g/3 oz button onions
5 sprigs of rosemary
salt and freshly milled pepper

Serves 4

Cut each quail along the backbone and bone out each bird very carefully without perforating the skin (see boning a duck, page 205). Season the inside with salt and pepper. Use a little of the stuffing to fill each quail, then reshape and sew back to the original shape with a trussing needle and string.

Chop up the bones and roast with the oil at 220°C/425°F/gas mark 7 for about 10 minutes. Add the mirepoix and roast for a further 10 minutes. Discard the fat. Add half the wine, the jus de veau and peppercorns to the roasting tin and simmer for about 20 minutes, skimming frequently. Pass through a fine sieve, reduce to the required consistency and season to taste. Stir in 25 g/1 oz of the butter.

Butter a shallow ovenproof dish and rub the inside with the garlic, then layer the slices of potato, seasoning with nutmeg, salt and pepper, and sprinkling with Gruyère. Continue until the dish is full and finish with a layer of Gruyère. Bring the cream to the boil, season with salt and pepper, pour over the potato and bake at 180°C/350°F/gas mark 4 for about 45 minutes, until tender.

Season the quails and roast at 220°C/425°F/gas mark 7 for about 20 minutes, basting frequently. Leave to rest for about 10 minutes.

Heat 25 g/1 oz of the butter and the sugar in a saucepan and caramelise. Add the button onions and the remaining white wine and simmer until all the liquid has evaporated. Add a small amount of the sauce and reduce until the onions are tender and evenly glazed. Add the leaves from one sprig of rosemary.

Remove the strings from the quails. Arrange some potatoes on each plate, position a quail on one side with some button onions and pour some sauce over each portion. Fry the remaining sprigs of rosemary in the remaining butter and use to garnish each plate.

CANON DE CHEVREUIL FARCI AUX ABRICOTS

LOIN OF VENISON WITH APRICOT FILLING

4 × 165 g / 5½ oz portions of loin of venison, trimmed	
275 ml / 9 fl oz red wine	
40 g / 1½ oz mirepoix (page 207)	
24 peppercorns, crushed	
½ bay leaf	
1 sprig of thyme	
1 juniper berry	
225 g / 8 oz dried apricots, soaked in cold water for at least 1 hour	
20 g / ¾ oz shallot, finely chopped	
120 g / 4½ oz unsalted butter	
50 g / 2 oz fresh white breadcrumbs, sieved	
10 g / ¼ oz freshly chopped herbs	
500 g / 1 lb 2 oz onions, very finely chopped	
50 ml / 2 fl oz oil	
25 ml / 1 fl oz red wine vinegar	
200 ml / 7 fl oz Grenadine	
200 ml / 7 fl oz game stock (page 196)	
100 ml / 3½ fl oz jus de veau (page 197)	
100 ml / 3½ fl oz double cream	
100 g / 4 oz chanterelles, cleaned	
salt and freshly milled pepper	
4 sprigs of mint	

Serves 4

Marinate the venison in 200 ml / 7 fl oz of the red wine with the mirepoix, peppercorns, bay leaf, thyme and juniper berry for two days. Remove from the marinade and strain the marinade, reserving the mirepoix and wine for the sauce.

Drain and dice the apricots. Sweat about one-third of the shallot in 15 g / ½ oz of the butter until transparent. Add the apricots, breadcrumbs and half the herbs. Season with salt and pepper. Make a cavity through the centre of each portion of venison using a sharpening steel and fill with the apricot stuffing.

Sweat the onions in half the oil and 25 g / 1 oz of the butter until transparent. Add the red wine vinegar and remaining wine, and reduce. Add the Grenadine and reduce until the liquid has completely evaporated and the onions are very soft. Spoon the mixture into four timbales or egg cups.

Season the portions of venison with salt and pepper. Heat the remaining oil and 25 g / 1 oz of the butter and seal the meat on all sides. Roast at 220°C / 425°F / gas mark 7 for 6–7 minutes. Remove from the pan, discard the fat, add the mirepoix and sweat in 15 g / ½ oz of the butter. Add the marinade and reduce by two-thirds. Add the game stock and jus de veau, and reduce to the required consistency. Add the cream, reduce and stir in 15 g / ½ oz of the butter. Season to taste, pass through a fine sieve or muslin and add the remaining herbs.

Sweat the remaining shallot in the remaining butter. Add the chanterelles and sweat for a further 2 minutes. Season with salt and pepper.

Unmould the onion timbales and position one on each plate. Add the chanterelles to the sauce and pour a little on each plate. Cut each portion of venison in 1-cm / ½-inch thick slices and arrange on top of the sauce. Garnish each onion timbale with a sprig of mint.

Serve with Spetzli (page 184).

DELICE DE ROUGE D'ECOSSE GASTRONOME

GROUSE WITH SAVOY CABBAGE

2 grouse, dressed
65 g/2½ oz chicken mousse (page 206)
2 leeks, cooked
50 ml/2 fl oz oil
50 g/2 oz mirepoix (page 207)
1 clove of garlic, crushed
1 sprig of thyme
1 bay leaf
12 peppercorns, crushed
100 ml/3½ fl oz red wine
200 ml/7 fl oz jus de veau (page 197)
10 g/¼ oz shallot, chopped
50 g/2 oz unsalted butter
75 g/3 oz assorted wild mushrooms, cleaned
freshly chopped parsley
200 g/7 oz Chou Frisé à la crème (page 180)
salt and freshly milled pepper
4 heart-shaped croûtons (page 195)

Serves 4

Remove the legs and wish-bones from the grouse and reserve. Remove the breasts, trim and remove the fillets. Split by making a cut horizontally almost through each one. Open out and place all the pieces of grouse between sheets of plastic and beat lightly to flatten (see chicken suprême, page 192). Season with salt and pepper. Spread some of the chicken mousse about 3-mm/⅛-inch thick on to each breast, leaving a 5-mm/¼-inch wide border.

Dry the leeks on a kitchen cloth and cut in 4-cm/1½-inch lengths. Place some in the centre of each grouse breast. Top each one with the reserved fillet and fold the pointed end and the sides over the leek to form a neat parcel. Wrap in clingfilm and steam for about 8 minutes until pink.

Chop the grouse legs and carcasses. Roast with the oil at 220°C/425°F/gas mark 7 for about 10 minutes. Add the mirepoix, garlic, thyme, bay leaf and peppercorns, and roast for a further 10 minutes. Discard the fat and add the red wine. Reduce, add the jus de veau and simmer for about 20 minutes, skimming frequently. Pass through a fine sieve, reduce to the required consistency, season to taste and stir in 25 g/1 oz of the butter.

Sweat the shallot in 25 g/1 oz of the butter until transparent, add the wild mushrooms, season to taste and add a sprinkling of chopped parsley.

Arrange some of the cabbage on each plate. Remove the clingfilm from the grouse and cut each one at an angle in four even slices. Place the slices of grouse on top of the cabbage. Spoon a little sauce over the slices of grouse and garnish with the wild mushrooms and heart-shaped croûtons, dipped in chopped parsley.

DELICE DE PIGEONNEAU FARCI PERIGUEUX

STUFFED PIGEONS

Remove the wish-bone and legs from each pigeon, carefully remove the breasts and chop up the bones and legs. Trim the breasts and make an incision with a long, narrow-bladed knife through the centre of each breast, starting at the thick end and working right down to the pointed end to form a pocket.

Cut the foie gras in four batons, season with salt and pepper and insert one in each breast. Wrap each breast carefully in caul.

Roast the pigeon bones in half the oil at 220°C/425°F/gas mark 7 for about 20 minutes or until brown, then add the mirepoix and cook for a further 10 minutes.

Discard the fat. Add the Madeira, truffle juice and jus de veau. Simmer for about 20 minutes, skimming frequently. Pass through fine muslin, reduce to the desired consistency and

4 pigeons, dressed
40 g/1½ oz fresh foie gras
65 g/2½ oz caul
25 ml/1 fl oz oil
50 g/2 oz mirepoix (page 207)
100 ml/3½ fl oz Madeira
100 ml/3½ fl oz truffle juice (page 198)
200 ml/7 fl oz jus de veau (page 197)
10 g/¼ oz truffle, chopped
150 g/5 oz kohlrabi
400 g/14 oz courgettes
300 ml/½ pint double cream
65 g/2½ oz Gruyère, grated
40 g/1½ oz unsalted butter
salt and freshly milled pepper

Serves 4

add the chopped truffle.

Cut the kohlrabi and courgettes in batons about 4-cm/1½-inch long, discarding the seeds from the courgettes. Cook the vegetables separately in boiling salted water until just tender and refresh.

Reduce the cream, add the vegetables, season with salt and pepper and add the Gruyère at the last moment.

Heat half the butter and the remaining oil and fry the pigeon breasts very quickly for about 2 minutes on each side until pink, then remove from the pan. Discard the fat in the pan and add the sauce.

Arrange some of the kohlrabi and courgette mixture on each of four plates and glaze under a hot grill. Lay two pigeon breasts on top of each portion. Stir the remaining butter into the sauce and season to taste. Spoon a little sauce over the pigeon breasts.

SUPREME DE FAISAN POMPADOUR

PHEASANT POMPADOUR

Remove the legs, wish-bones, skin and winglets from the pheasants. Bone out the thighs and use the meat to prepare pheasant mousse (see below). Remove the breasts from the carcasses, and remove and reserve the fillets from each breast. Spread a little of the pheasant mousse on each breast and replace the fillet.

Chop the carcasses and roast with half the oil at 220°C/425°F/gas mark 7 for 10–15 minutes. Add the mirepoix and roast for a further 5 minutes.

Add the white wine, game stock, jus de veau, crushed peppercorns, bay leaf and sprig of thyme. Simmer for about 10 minutes, skimming frequently. Pass through a fine sieve or muslin.

Fry the breasts of pheasant in the remaining oil and half the butter until pink. Remove the breasts and keep in a warm place.

2 pheasants, dressed

200 g/7 oz pheasant mousse (see below)

50 ml/2 fl oz oil

40 g/1½ oz mirepoix (page 207)

100 ml/3½ fl oz dry white wine

100 ml/3½ fl oz game stock (page 196)

200 ml/7 fl oz jus de veau (page 197)

12 peppercorns, crushed

½ bay leaf

1 sprig of thyme

50 g/2 oz unsalted butter

100 ml/3½ fl oz brown ale

5 ml/1 teaspoon cumin seeds

4 Rösti de Panais et Carottes (page 188)

200 g/7 oz swede, turned in long cylindrical shapes and cooked al dente

200 g/7 oz kohlrabi, turned in long cylindrical shapes and cooked al dente

200 g/7 oz carrots, turned in long cylindrical shapes and cooked al dente

100 g/4 oz small Brussels sprouts, cooked al dente

75 g/3 oz streaky bacon, cut in lardons and blanched

freshly chopped parsley

salt and freshly milled pepper

Serves 4

Discard the fat, add the brown ale and reduce almost completely. Add the sauce and reduce to the required consistency. Mix the cumin seeds with a small amount of the remaining butter and chop very finely. Add to the sauce and simmer for about 5 minutes.

Place a Rösti de Panais et Carottes on each plate. Arrange a breast of pheasant on top and pour a little sauce over each portion.

Melt the remaining butter and toss the bacon lardons until crisp, then toss all the vegetables quickly. Sprinkle with chopped parsley, season with salt and pepper, and use to garnish the pheasant.

PHEASANT MOUSSE: Use the meat from the pheasant thighs; otherwise follow the recipe for chicken mousse (page 206).

PERDREAU MAURICE BRAISE AUX MARRONS

MAURICE'S PARTRIDGE BRAISED WITH CHESTNUTS

Cut each partridge in half and season with salt and pepper.

Heat the oil and 25 g/1 oz of the butter and fry the partridges until brown on all sides. Remove from the pan and discard the fat.

Add 25 g/1 oz of the butter to the pan and sweat the mirepoix. Add the port and reduce. Add the game stock, jus de veau, peppercorns, thyme and bay leaf.

Place the partridges in an ovenproof dish, add the sauce, cover and braise at 180°C/350°F/gas mark 4 for 12–15 minutes. Remove the partridges and remove the breast bones.

Pass the sauce through a fine sieve or muslin. Bring to the boil, skim any fat from the surface, season to taste and stir in half the remaining butter.

Ingredient
4 partridges, dressed
25 ml/1 fl oz oil
75 g/3 oz unsalted butter
40 g/1½ oz mirepoix (page 207)
100 ml/3½ fl oz ruby port
200 ml/7 fl oz game stock (page 196)
200 ml/7 fl oz jus de veau (page 197)
24 peppercorns, crushed
1 sprig of thyme
½ bay leaf
10 g/¼ oz caster sugar
100 ml/3½ fl oz dry white wine
150 g/5 oz chestnuts
200 g/7 oz Chou Frisé à la crème (page 180)
200 g/7 oz Chou Rouge Braisé (page 184)
salt and freshly milled pepper

Serves 4

Place the remaining butter and the sugar in a saucepan and caramelise. Pour in the white wine and reduce.

Make a cross-shaped incision with a small knife in each chestnut, place on a baking tray and roast at 230°C/450°F/gas mark 8 until the cut points curl up. Remove the skins.

Place the chestnuts in the wine reduction and reduce until the liquid has evaporated, then add about 50 ml/2 fl oz of the sauce. Reduce until the chestnuts are evenly coated and the sauce becomes a thick syrup.

Place a small amount of the green and red cabbage on each plate. Place half a partridge on each portion of cabbage.

Garnish with chestnuts and spoon some sauce over each portion.

LES
DESSERTS

GATEAU DE CYGNES A LA SAVOY

SAVOY SWAN GATEAU

Even in the annals of The Savoy, no party can rival the spectacular Gondola Dinner given by the American millionaire George A Kessler in July 1905 to celebrate his birthday. The guests dined in an enormous gondola floating in the old courtyard which had been flooded to a depth of several feet. Caruso sang arias as this gâteau was served.

150 g/5 oz choux paste (page 194)
25 g/1 oz caster sugar
750 ml/1¼ pints double cream
icing sugar
1 round Genoese sponge, 20-cm/8-inch diameter (page 197)
40 ml/1½ fl oz Kirsch
40 ml/1½ fl oz sugar syrup (page 204)
100 g/4 oz raspberries
50 g/2 oz nibbed almonds, roasted
50 g/2 oz plain chocolate couverture, tempered (page 204)

Serves 10

Using a 1-cm/½-inch plain nozzle, pipe ten 2.5-cm/1-inch rounds of choux paste on to a buttered baking tray. Bake at 200°C/400°F/gas mark 6 for 15 minutes.

Using a 3-mm/⅛-inch plain nozzle, pipe ten 'S' shapes in choux paste on to a buttered baking tray. Bake at 180°C/350°F/gas mark 4 for 10 minutes until crisp and golden.

Split the buns horizontally and then cut the tops in half.

Add the caster sugar to the cream and whip until just firm.

To assemble the swans, use a small star nozzle to fill the bases of the choux buns with some of the cream. Place the top halves at an angle to give the impression of wings. Place an 'S'-shaped piece of choux paste in front of each bun for the neck. Dust each swan with icing sugar.

Slice the Genoese sponge horizontally into three equal layers and moisten each with a little Kirsch and sugar syrup. Place the first layer on a cake board or plate. Spread with some of the remaining cream and sprinkle with a few raspberries. Repeat with the next layer and top with the third layer of sponge.

Spread the top and sides of the sponge carefully with the remaining cream and run a comb scraper around the sides to give a decorative effect. Press the nibbed almonds on to the sides of the gâteau.

Pour the chocolate on to a plate and leave to set. Pull a metal spoon over the surface of the chocolate to form curls. Arrange these in the centre of the gâteau. Position the swans with the heads pointing inwards.

BRULEE D'ORANGE ET SA JULIENNE

BURNT ORANGE CREAM

350 ml / 12 fl oz double cream
4 egg yolks
50 g / 2 oz caster sugar
1 vanilla pod
100 g / 4 oz orange segments (page 203)
20 g / ¾ oz caramelised orange julienne (page 193)
40 ml / 1½ fl oz Grand Marnier
25 g / 1 oz icing sugar

Serves 4

Mix the cream, egg yolks and caster sugar together and pass through a fine sieve. Remove the seeds from the vanilla pod and stir into the cream mixture.

Divide the orange segments between four ramekins and scatter the caramelised orange julienne on top.

Add the Grand Marnier and divide the cream mixture between the ramekins. Cook at 150°C/300°F/gas mark 2 in a bain-Marie for about 40 minutes until lightly set. Leave to cool.

Dust with the icing sugar and glaze under a hot grill to give a golden brown caramelised top.

JALOUSIE AUX FRUITS EN SAISON ET DEUX COULIS

FRUIT JALOUSIE

250 g/9 oz puff paste (page 200)

120 g/4½ oz frangipane (page 196)

10 large apricot halves, poached and well drained

50 g/2 oz Griottine cherries, well drained

1 egg yolk, beaten

apricot jam, sieved and warmed

icing sugar

Serves 10

Roll out the puff paste about 3-mm/ ⅛-inch thick and cut two 50 × 10-cm/20 × 4-inch strips. Place one strip on a buttered baking tray. Using a 1-cm/½-inch plain nozzle, pipe two lines of frangipane down the centre of this strip. Mark the second strip with a lattice roller.

Arrange the apricots and cherries alternately on top of the frangipane.

Brush the edges with egg yolk and carefully position the lattice strip on top. Seal the edges well, brush the surface of the paste with egg yolk and bake at 200°C/400°F/gas mark 6 for about 20 minutes until crisp and golden.

Brush carefully with apricot jam glaze and dust the edges with icing sugar. Serve with strawberry and vanilla sauces (pages 201 and 205).

DEMI-MANGUE ET SA GLACE DIANA

MANGO FILLED WITH ICE CREAM

2 medium-sized, ripe mangoes
400 ml/14 fl oz vanilla ice cream mixture (page 205)
50 ml/2 fl oz raspberry sauce (page 201)
50 ml/2 fl oz mango sauce (page 198)
12 raspberries
24 wild strawberries
4 sprigs of mint

Serves 4

Cut the mangoes in half lengthways, removing the stones carefully with a spoon. Scoop out most of the flesh and chill the skins.

Purée the mango in a blender and then pass through a fine sieve. Add the mango purée to the vanilla ice cream mixture and freeze to a piping consistency.

Using a small paper piping bag, pipe a ring of raspberry sauce around the edge of each plate. Pipe an inner ring of mango sauce. Bring the two rings together with a cocktail stick to give a feathered design.

Using a large star nozzle pipe the mango ice cream into the chilled mango skins and position one in the centre of each plate. Decorate the top of each with three raspberries, six wild strawberries and a sprig of mint. Serve with palmiers (page 200).

TERRINE DE FRUITS D'ETE

TERRINE OF SUMMER FRUITS

8 leaves of gelatine, soaked in cold water
750 ml/1¼ pints sugar syrup (page 204)
40 ml/1½ fl oz Kirsch
100 g/4 oz wild strawberries
100 g/4 oz blueberries
100 g/4 oz raspberries
150 g/5 oz tayberries
450 ml/¾ pint lime sauce (page 197)

Serves 10

Drain the excess water from the gelatine, then dissolve over a gentle heat in the sugar syrup. Leave to cool, then stir in the Kirsch.

Arrange a layer of wild strawberries in the base of a 1.25-litre/2¼-pint terrine. Pour on sufficient syrup to just cover, then chill until set. Repeat the layering until all the fruit and syrup have been used, leaving each layer to set before adding the next. Chill the terrine until completely firm.

Cut the terrine in slices and position a slice on each plate. Pour a little lime sauce around each portion.

Other summer fruits may also be used, if desired.

PETIT GATEAU DE REINETTE A MA FACON

**APPLE CAKE WITH
ORANGE SABAYON SAUCE**

50 g/2 oz unsalted butter
175 g/6 oz sweet paste (page 204)
2 small Reinette apples, peeled, cored and thinly sliced
200 ml/7 fl oz soured cream
90 g/3½ oz caster sugar
65 g/2½ oz plain flour
1 egg
a few drops of vanilla extract
25 g/1 oz walnuts, chopped
25 g/1 oz brown sugar
ground cinnamon
salt
icing sugar
50 ml/2 fl oz orange juice
50 ml/2 fl oz lemon juice
4 egg yolks
300 ml/½ pint Marsala

Serves 4

Use half the butter to coat the inside of four individual ramekins (about 9-cm/3½-inch diameter and 4-cm/1½-inch high). Roll out the sweet paste 3-mm/⅛-inch thick and use to line the ramekins. Fill the ramekins with the apple slices.

Whisk the soured cream with 25 g/1 oz of the caster sugar, half the flour and the egg. Pass through a fine sieve and flavour with vanilla extract. Cover the apple with this mixture. Bake at 190°C/375°F/gas mark 5 for 10 minutes.

Combine the chopped walnuts, remaining flour, brown sugar, a little cinnamon and a pinch of salt. Melt the remaining butter and mix with the dry ingredients to form a crumb texture. Sprinkle a little on top of each ramekin and bake for a further 10 minutes.

Leave to cool slightly, then turn out on to individual warm plates and dust with icing sugar.

Whisk the orange and lemon juices, egg yolks, remaining caster sugar and Marsala over boiling water until the sauce becomes light and fluffy. Pour the sauce around each portion. Serve raspberry sauce (page 201) separately.

PECHE A LA MELBA EN CAGE

PEACH MELBA

2 large peaches
600 ml/1 pint sugar syrup (page 204)
250 g/9 oz caster sugar
100 ml/3½ fl oz water
10 g/¼ oz glucose
300 ml/½ pint raspberry sauce (page 201)
4 tulip baskets (page 172)
400 ml/14 fl oz vanilla ice cream (page 205)

Serves 4

Poach the peaches in the sugar syrup for 1 minute until the skin comes off easily. Peel, leave to cool, then cut in half and remove the stones.

Mix the sugar, water and glucose together in a small saucepan and place over a high heat. Brush the sides of the pan quite frequently with a little water to prevent any crystallisation. Cook the sugar to the hard crack stage (152°C/310°F on a sugar thermometer). Leave to cool until the syrup becomes thick.

Oil the outside of a 10-cm/4-inch diameter ladle. Dip two dessert forks in the sugar syrup and flick very fine threads over the upturned ladle, changing the direction of the threads to form a lattice effect. Turn the ladle on its side and finish with a thin line of sugar syrup around the edge of the ladle to form the base of the cage. As soon as it is cool, carefully remove the cage from the ladle and keep in a cool, dry place. Make three more cages in the same way.

Pour a little of the raspberry sauce on to each of four plates. Place a tulip basket in the centre of each plate. Scoop a quarter of the vanilla ice cream in the centre and set a peach half on top. Spoon over a little raspberry sauce. Carefully arrange a sugar cage on top of each tulip basket.

PETIT GATEAU DE FROMAGE CHAUD AU COULIS AUX FRUITS

WARM CHEESECAKE WITH FRUIT SAUCES

175 g/6 oz sweet paste (page 204)
120 g/4½ oz low-fat soft cheese
50 g/2 oz caster sugar
few drops of vanilla extract
pinch of salt
10 g/¼ oz cornflour
2 egg yolks
100 ml/3½ fl oz double cream
grated rind of 1 lemon
juice of ½ lemon
1 egg white
icing sugar
100 ml/3½ fl oz mango sauce (page 198)
100 ml/3½ fl oz strawberry sauce (page 201)
4 strawberries, chopped
75 g/3 oz mango, diced

Serves 4

Roll out the sweet paste 3-mm/ ⅛-inch thick and use to line four buttered ramekins.

Mix the soft cheese and caster sugar together. Add the vanilla extract, salt, cornflour, egg yolks, cream, lemon rind and lemon juice, and stir to a smooth consistency. Whisk the egg white to a stiff peak and fold into the soft cheese mixture. Use this to fill the prepared ramekins and bake at 180°C/ 350°F/gas mark 4 for 30–35 minutes until lightly set and golden brown. Leave to cool slightly, then turn out and dust with icing sugar.

Swirl a quarter of the mango sauce in a spiral design on to each plate. Fill the remaining space with the strawberry sauce. Position a small cheesecake in the centre of each plate and sprinkle the sauces with the chopped strawberries and diced mango.

FONDANT DE CHOCOLAT, SAUCE DE NOISETTES AU COINTREAU

CHILLED CHOCOLATE FONDANT

450 ml/¾ pint vanilla sauce (page 205)
75 g/3 oz hazelnuts, roasted, skinned and ground
50 ml/2 fl oz Cointreau
120 g/4½ oz vanilla sponge (page 205)
5 egg yolks
50 g/2 oz caster sugar
50 ml/2 fl oz brandy
175 g/6 oz plain chocolate couverture, tempered (page 204)
600 ml/1 pint double cream, lightly whipped
caramelised orange julienne (page 193)
10 fresh mint leaves

Serves 10

Warm the vanilla sauce and stir in the hazelnuts. Leave to stand for 1 hour and then pass through a fine sieve. Add the Cointreau.

Line the base and sides of a 1.25-litre/2¼-pint terrine neatly with very thin slices of the vanilla sponge.

Whisk the egg yolks and sugar over hot water until thick and pale. Stir in the brandy and 150 g/5 oz of the chocolate. Pass the chocolate mixture through a fine sieve and keep warm. Gently fold in the cream and pour into the prepared terrine.

Freeze for about 2 hours or until firm but not frozen. Carefully turn out the fondant and cut in 2-cm/¾-inch thick slices.

Divide the hazelnut sauce between ten plates. Place a slice of the chocolate fondant in the centre and decorate each slice with a little caramelised orange julienne and a mint leaf. Pipe the remaining chocolate around the hazelnut sauce and feather it, using a cocktail stick.

PETIT PARFAIT
DE NOËL

CHRISTMAS PARFAIT

2 egg yolks
50 g/2 oz caster sugar
25 ml/1 fl oz Crème de Menthe
400 ml/14 fl oz double cream
25 g/1 oz plain chocolate couverture, tempered (page 204)
25 g/1 oz white chocolate couverture, tempered
100 ml/3½ fl oz chocolate sauce (page 194)
150 ml/¼ pint orange sauce (page 200)
400 g/14 oz Griottine cherries in brandy
10 ml/2 teaspoons arrowroot
4 sprigs of mint

Serves 4

Whisk the egg yolks, half the sugar and the Crème de Menthe over boiling water to form a light, fluffy sabayon. Leave to cool and pass through a fine sieve.

Reserve 150 ml/¼ pint of the cream. Lightly whip the remainder and fold into the cold sabayon. Spoon this mixture into a half-circle sleeve mould lined with clingfilm. Level the surface with a palette knife, cover with clingfilm and freeze for about 4 hours or until firm.

Unmould the parfait. Whip the reserved cream and spread evenly over the parfait. Pull a comb scraper across the cream to give a lined effect. Freeze for a further 30 minutes.

Fill a small paper piping bag with the plain chocolate and pipe four small Christmas tree run-outs on to baking parchment. Before the chocolate sets, fill the centre of each tree with a little of the white chocolate, making it run into the outline. Leave to set.

Pipe four gates in plain chocolate on to baking parchment. Leave to set.

Pipe three loops of plain chocolate on to each plate. Leave to set. Then fill the run-out design with chocolate sauce. Pipe white chocolate into the centre of each loop and feather it with a cocktail stick.

Mix the arrowroot with a little cherry juice. Heat the cherries in brandy, add the arrowroot mixture and cook over a gentle heat until slightly thickened.

Pour a little orange sauce around the edge of each plate and decorate with some of the cherries.

Cut the parfait in neat portions with a sharp, warm knife and arrange a slice at the top of the design. Position the chocolate run-outs on the top and decorate with the sprigs of mint. Serve the remaining hot cherries separately in a sauceboat.

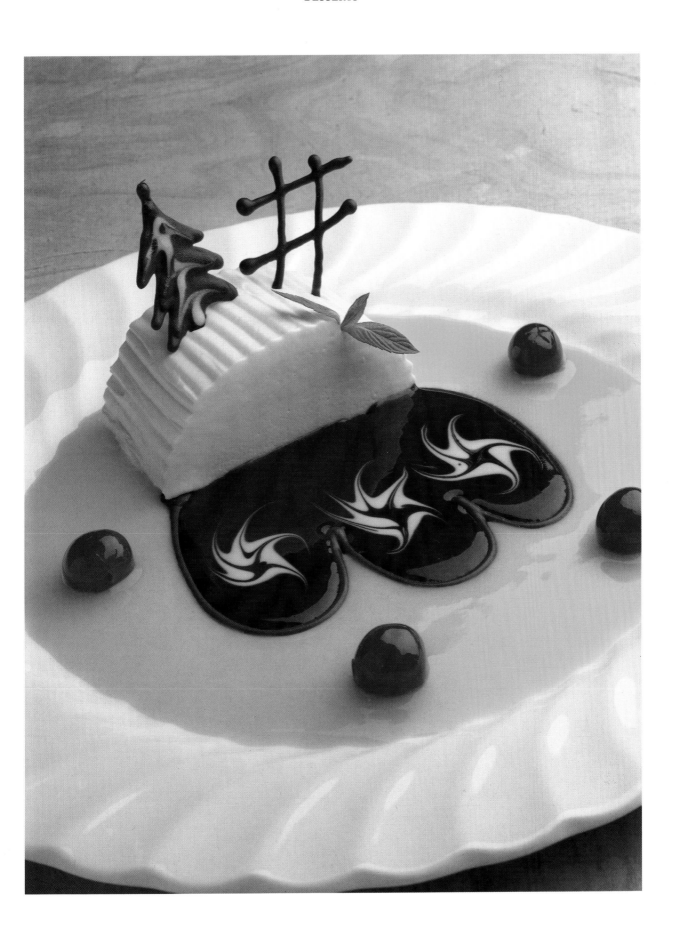

PETITE BOMBE GLACÉE PAQUITA

ICED BOMBE PAQUITA

3 egg yolks
40 ml/1½ fl oz Anisette
250 g/9 oz caster sugar
200 ml/7 fl oz double cream
25 g/1 oz hazelnuts, roasted, skinned and finely chopped
20 g/¾ oz vanilla sponge (page 205)
25 ml/1 fl oz Kirsch
4 egg whites
50 g/2 oz orange segments
50 g/2 oz paw paw, turned
50 g/2 oz kiwi, turned

Serves 4

Whisk the egg yolks, Anisette and 40 g/1½ oz of the sugar over boiling water to form a light, fluffy sabayon. Then pass through a fine sieve and leave to cool. Lightly whip the cream and fold in the hazelnuts and sabayon. Spoon this mixture into four dariole moulds (about 5-cm/2-inch diameter and 7.5-cm/3-inch high). Cover with clingfilm and freeze until firm.

Cut the vanilla sponge into four 5-cm/2-inch rounds and moisten with the Kirsch. Dip the dariole moulds into hot water and unmould the parfaits on to the sponge rounds. Position on chilled plates and place in the freezer.

Whisk the egg whites until stiff, then whisk in the remaining sugar, a spoonful at a time until the mixture is thick and glossy. Using a small star nozzle, pipe the meringue up the sides of each parfait to cover completely. Glaze evenly under a hot grill until light golden brown.

Arrange the fruit on the plate. Serve with raspberry sauce (page 201).

POIRE
SOUS SA CROUTE

PEAR IN PASTRY LATTICE

2 fresh pears, peeled and cored
500 ml/18 fl oz sugar syrup (page 204)
225 g/8 oz puff paste (page 200)
75 g/3 oz frangipane (page 196)
1 egg yolk, beaten
25 g/1 oz icing sugar
50 ml/2 fl oz Poire William
300 ml/½ pint vanilla sauce (page 205)

Serves 4

Poach the pears gently in the sugar syrup. Leave to cool, then cut in half.

Roll out half the puff paste about 3-mm/⅛-inch thick and cut out four pear shapes slightly larger than the poached pear halves. Place the paste shapes on a buttered baking tray and pipe a little frangipane in the centre of each. Position the poached pear halves on top.

Roll out the remaining puff paste thinly and mark with a lattice roller. Brush the edges of the puff paste shapes with egg yolk and stretch the lattice over the top of each one. Seal the edges and trim neatly. Leave to rest for 20 minutes.

Brush the lattice with egg yolk and bake at 190°C/375°F/gas mark 5 for about 15 minutes until golden brown. Dust with icing sugar and glaze carefully under a hot grill.

Add the Poire William to the vanilla sauce and warm gently.

Place a pear on each plate and pour some sauce around.

SUMMER PUDDING

**SHOWN IN ENGLISH
ON SAVOY MENUS**

175 g/6 oz white bread, thinly sliced and crusts removed
150 g/5 oz strawberries
150 g/5 oz blueberries
50 g/2 oz raspberries
50 g/2 oz red currants
50 g/2 oz caster sugar
300 ml/½ pint blackcurrant sauce (page 192)
double cream, whipped
4 wild strawberries
16 blueberries
12 raspberries
4 sprigs of red currant
4 sprigs of blackcurrant
icing sugar

Serves 4

Line the base and sides of four dariole moulds with most of the bread by cutting it in 1-cm (½-inch) wide fingers.

Simmer all the berries with the sugar over a moderate heat for about 10 minutes until the fruit is tender and the syrup is slightly reduced.

Pour the hot fruit and syrup into the bread-lined moulds. Allow the bread to soak up the syrup, then add extra fruit as necessary to fill each mould completely. Top each with a round of bread slightly smaller than the mould. Cover and chill overnight.

Unmould each summer pudding on to a plate. Spoon some blackcurrant sauce over each pudding and decorate with a rosette of cream and a wild strawberry. Decorate each plate with four blueberries, three raspberries and a sprig of both red currant and blackcurrant dusted with icing sugar.

TARTE
AUX ABRICOTS

APRICOT TART

12 fresh apricots, halved and stones removed	
600 ml/1 pint sugar syrup (page 204)	
200 g/7 oz sweet paste (page 204)	
50 g/2 oz Genoese sponge (page 197)	
40 ml/1½ fl oz Kirsch	
150 ml/¼ pint pastry cream (page 200)	
19 whole almonds, roasted and skinned	
75 ml/3 fl oz apricot jam, warmed and sieved	
25 g/1 oz pistachio nuts, finely chopped	

Serves 8

Poach the apricot halves in the sugar syrup until just tender. Drain thoroughly and leave to cool.

Roll out the sweet paste 3-mm/ ⅛-inch thick and use to line a 20-cm/ 8-inch flan ring. Bake blind at 190°C/ 375°F/gas mark 5 for about 20 minutes until lightly golden.

Whilst still warm, transfer the flan case to a plate. Leave to cool.

Arrange a thin layer of Genoese sponge on the base of the flan case.

Moisten with the Kirsch. Top with a layer of pastry cream. Arrange the apricot halves, cut side up, in the flan case, ensuring that the pastry cream is completely covered.

Cut small slices of the remaining apricot and arrange to finish the edge of the tart decoratively. Place a whole roasted almond in each apricot half. Lightly glaze with the warm jam. Decorate the edge of the flan with the chopped pistachio nuts.

TARTE BOURDALOUE

BOURDALOUE TART

200 g/7 oz sweet paste (page 204)
100 g/4 oz ground almonds
25 g/1 oz plain flour
100 g/4 oz caster sugar
100 ml/3½ fl oz egg white
25 g/1 oz unsalted butter
50 ml/2 fl oz Poire William
4 small pears, peeled and cored
1 litre/1¾ pints sugar syrup (page 204)
50 g/2 oz apricot jam, warmed and sieved
icing sugar

Serves 8

Roll out the sweet paste 3-mm/ ⅛-inch thick and use to line a 20-cm/ 8-inch flan ring. Trim the edges carefully.

Mix the ground almonds, flour, sugar and egg white to a smooth consistency. Melt the butter over a high heat until it turns nut brown in colour, then quickly stir into the almond mixture. Stir in the Poire William.

Lightly poach the pears in the sugar syrup until just tender. Leave to cool, drain well and cut in half.

Spread the almond mixture over the base of the flan case and arrange the pear halves on top, keeping the curved surfaces uppermost.

Bake at 170°C/325°F/gas mark 3 for about 45 minutes until golden brown and just firm.

Remove the flan ring and lightly glaze the surface with the apricot jam. Dust the edge of the flan with icing sugar. Serve immediately, accompanied by warm vanilla sauce (page 205).

TARTELETTE AUX PRUNEAUX, SABAYON A L'ORANGE

PLUM TARTLET WITH ORANGE SABAYON SAUCE

200 g / 7 oz puff paste (page 200)
50 ml / 2 fl oz pastry cream (page 200)
300 g / 10 oz plums, halved, stoned and thinly sliced
20 g / ¾ oz plain flour
15 g / ½ oz brown sugar
15 g / ½ oz walnuts, chopped
ground cinnamon
15 g / ½ oz unsalted butter, melted
5 egg yolks
75 g / 3 oz caster sugar
100 ml / 3½ fl oz Sauternes
50 ml / 2 fl oz lemon juice
50 ml / 2 fl oz orange juice

Serves 4

Roll out the puff paste thinly and stamp out four 12.5-cm / 5-inch rounds. Place on a buttered baking tray, prick thoroughly with a fork and leave to rest in the refrigerator for 30 minutes.

Spread a thin layer of pastry cream over each pastry round. Neatly fan the plum slices out on to the pastry rounds.

Mix the flour, brown sugar, walnuts, a generous pinch of cinnamon and the butter together. Sprinkle over the plums and bake at 180°C / 350°F / gas mark 4 for about 20 minutes until golden brown.

Whisk together the egg yolks, caster sugar, Sauternes, and lemon and orange juices over boiling water to form a light, fluffy sabayon. Spoon a little on to each warm plate. Place the tartlets in the centre of the sabayon.

TULIPE DE SORBET
AUX FRUITS D'ETE

TULIP BASKET FILLED WITH
SUMMER FRUITS AND SORBET

Place an eight-pointed 12.5-cm/ 5-inch diameter star-shaped plastic stencil on a buttered and floured baking tray. Spread a little tuile mixture in the centre and draw a palette knife evenly over the surface. Remove the stencil and make three more stars in the same way.

Sprinkle a few flaked almonds in the centre of each star. Bake at 190°C/ 375°F/gas mark 5 for 4–5 minutes until light brown.

Whilst still hot, place each tuile in a small glass bowl to form a tulip basket. Leave in the bowls until cold and crisp.

Divide the raspberry sauce between four plates. Pipe three large spots of vanilla sauce around the edge of each

75 g/3 oz tuile mixture (page 205)
25 g/1 oz flaked almonds
225 g/8 oz summer berries to include raspberries, loganberries, wild strawberries, blackberries and blueberries
200 ml/7 fl oz raspberry sauce (page 201)
50 ml/2 fl oz vanilla sauce (page 205)
25 ml/1 fl oz mango sauce (page 198)
6 sprigs of red currant
6 sprigs of blackcurrant
icing sugar
250 ml/8 fl oz strawberry sorbet (page 201)
4 sprigs of mint

Serves 4

plate. Top each vanilla sauce spot with a small spot of mango sauce. With a cocktail stick, draw through the spots of sauce to give a leaf-shaped effect. Place a sprig of red currant or blackcurrant dusted with icing sugar between each.

Place a tulip basket in the centre of each plate and fill with the prepared fruit. Pipe some sorbet into the centre of each tulip basket and decorate with a sprig of mint.

Note: The sorbet in the photograph was made with elder flowers. As these are only available in early summer, strawberry sorbet is given in the recipe.

FEUILLETE
AUX FRUITS ROUGES

SUMMER FRUITS IN A PASTRY LEAF

250 g/9 oz puff paste (page 200)
1 egg yolk, beaten
150 ml/¼ pint pastry cream (page 200)
100 ml/3½ fl oz raspberry sauce (page 201)
150 g/5 oz raspberries
150 g/5 oz wild strawberries
icing sugar
200 ml/7 fl oz vanilla sauce (page 205)
40 ml/1½ fl oz Kirsch
25 ml/1 fl oz orange sauce (page 200)
4 sprigs of mint

Serves 4

Roll out the puff paste to 5-mm/ ¼-inch thick and cut out four leaf shapes. Place on a buttered baking tray and leave to rest in the refrigerator for 30 minutes.

Brush lightly with egg yolk. Using a small, sharp knife, score a line about 3 mm/¼ inch in from the edge of each leaf. Mark the inner part with the back of a knife to give a criss-cross pattern. Bake at 200°C/400°F/gas mark 6 for about 20 minutes until golden brown.

Carefully remove the lid of each leaf with a small knife and keep to one side. Scoop out any uncooked dough from the centre.

Mix the pastry cream with half the raspberry sauce, warm gently, then fill each pastry case with some of this mixture. Arrange the raspberries and wild strawberries on top, ensuring that the pastry cream is completely covered. Dust the edge of each pastry lid with a little icing sugar and place at an angle on top of the fruit.

Warm the vanilla sauce and add the Kirsch. Pour a thin layer on to each plate. Position a filled pastry case in the centre of each plate. Pipe three large dots of the remaining raspberry sauce on each plate. Pipe a small dot of orange sauce in the centre and, using a cocktail stick, feather through each dot several times. Decorate each feuilleté with a sprig of mint.

PETITE TARTE DESMOISELLES TATIN

APPLE UPSIDE-DOWN TART

100 g/4 oz caster sugar
400 ml/14 fl oz water
10 g/¼ oz glucose
7 medium dessert apples, peeled and cored
juice of ½ lemon
ground cinnamon
50 g/2 oz unsalted butter
100 g/4 oz puff paste (page 200)
4 sprigs of apple mint

Serves 4

Cook the sugar, water and glucose in a heavy-based saucepan to a pale amber colour. Put a little of this caramel on to the base of four individual ramekins (about 9-cm/3½-inch diameter and 4-cm/1½-inch high).

Slice the apples thinly and sprinkle with the lemon juice and a little cinnamon. Fill the ramekin dishes with the sliced apple and bake at 180°C/350°F/gas mark 4 for about 15 minutes until soft and reduced.

Sauté the remaining apple in the butter. Top up the ramekin dishes with this mixture and leave to cool.

Roll out the puff paste 3-mm/⅛-inch thick and cut into four rounds slightly larger than the top of each ramekin. Prick the puff paste with a fork and leave to rest for 20 minutes. Cover the ramekins of apple with the rounds of puff paste and bake at 190°C/375°F/gas mark 5 for 20 minutes.

Leave to cool slightly before turning each one on to a plate. Surround with warm vanilla sauce and decorate with sprigs of apple mint.

REINETTE EN CHAUSSON, BEURRE AU CALVADOS

**APPLE WRAPPED IN PASTRY
WITH CALVADOS BUTTER**

75 g/3 oz sultanas
25 ml/1 fl oz Calvados
4 Reinette apples
ground cinnamon
300 g/10 oz puff paste (page 200)
1 egg yolk, beaten
25 g/1 oz icing sugar
50 g/2 oz caster sugar
50 ml/2 fl oz water
10 g/¼ oz glucose
50 g/2 oz unsalted butter
150 ml/¼ pint double cream

Serves 4

Soak the sultanas in the Calvados for at least 1 hour. Drain, reserving the Calvados. Top and tail the apples so they stand level. Sprinkle the sultanas with the cinnamon and use to fill the centre of each apple.

Roll out the puff paste 3-mm/⅛-inch thick. Cut four ovals about 18 × 12.5-cm/7 × 5-inch and brush the edges with egg yolk. Enclose an apple in each oval of puff paste. Seal the edges well and crimp with a small knife. Brush each one with egg yolk and make a small cut in the top. Bake at 190°C/375°F/gas mark 5 for about 20 minutes. Remove from the oven and dust generously with icing sugar. Place under a hot grill to give a nice shiny glaze.

Cook the caster sugar, water and glucose in a heavy-based saucepan to a pale amber colour. Stir in the butter and the cream, reserving 25 ml/1 fl oz, then add the reserved Calvados. Pass through a fine sieve.

Position each apple on a warm plate and surround with the sauce. Feather with the reserved cream.

PARFAIT DE THE
AU COULIS DE CAFE

TEA PARFAIT WITH COFFEE SAUCE

2 egg yolks
25 g / 1 oz caster sugar
25 ml / 1 fl oz Marsala
50 ml / 2 fl oz sugar syrup (page 204)
5 ml (1 teaspoon) Earl Grey tea
600 ml / 1 pint double cream
50 ml / 2 fl oz raspberry sauce (page 201)
50 g / 2 oz plain chocolate couverture, tempered (page 204)
150 ml / ¼ pint coffee sauce (page 195)
25 ml / 1 fl oz chocolate sauce (page 194)
4 sprigs of mint

Serves 4

Whisk the egg yolks, sugar and Marsala over boiling water to form a light, fluffy sabayon. Pass through a fine sieve and leave to cool.

Heat the sugar syrup and infuse the tea leaves. Leave to cool and pass the syrup through a fine sieve.

Reserve 100 ml / 3½ fl oz of the cream. Fold the tea syrup into the sabayon and remaining cream. Spoon this mixture into a half circle sleeve mould lined with clingfilm. Level the surface, cover with clingfilm and freeze for 3–4 hours.

Unmould the parfait. Whip the reserved cream. Fold the raspberry sauce into two-thirds of the cream and spread over the parfait. Pull a comb scraper across the raspberry cream to give a lined effect. Freeze for a further 30 minutes.

Fill a small paper piping bag with the tempered chocolate and pipe several designs of small tea and coffee pots on to baking parchment. Leave to set.

Cut the parfait in neat portions with a sharp, warm knife.

Pour a little coffee sauce on to each plate. Position a slice of parfait in the centre of each plate. Pipe five large dots of chocolate sauce around each plate and add a dot of coffee sauce on top of each one. Draw through the dots with a cocktail stick. Decorate the top with a small rosette of the reserved whipped cream and a sprig of mint. Position the coffee and tea pot designs in the cream.

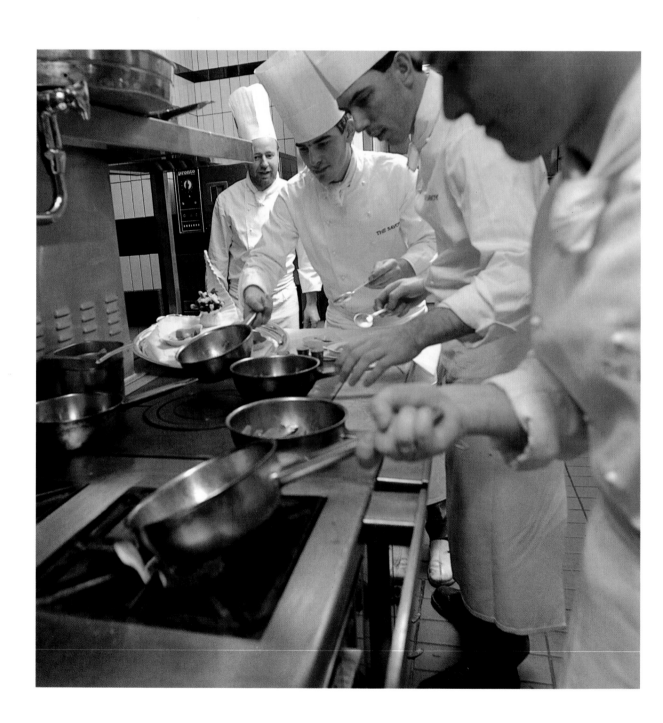

VEGETABLE
ACCOMPANIMENTS
AND GARNISHES

CHOU FRISE A LA CREME

SAVOY CABBAGE WITH CREAM	This dish is shown in the photograph on page 150	Serves 4–6

Remove the outside leaves from the cabbage and discard. Cut the cabbage in quarters, discard the stalk and shred very finely. Blanch in boiling salted water for about 4 minutes, refresh and squeeze out excess moisture.

1 × 750 g/1¾ lb Savoy cabbage
65 g/2½ oz streaky bacon, cut in julienne
20 g/¾ oz unsalted butter
300 ml/½ pint double cream
salt and freshly milled pepper

Blanch the streaky bacon for 30 seconds and refresh. Melt the butter and fry the bacon until crisp. Drain thoroughly. Reduce the cream by half and add the cabbage and bacon. Warm gently. Season to taste.

POMMES SAVOYARD

SAVOY POTATOES	This dish is shown in the photograph on page 121	Serves 4

Slice the potatoes about 3-mm/⅛-inch thick, then dry thoroughly on a kitchen cloth.

Heat the oil and toss the potato slices very quickly to blanch them. Season generously with salt and pepper and arrange neatly in four buttered 10-

300 g/10 oz potatoes, cut in small cylinders
25 ml/1 fl oz oil
20 g/¾ oz unsalted butter
salt and freshly milled pepper

cm/4-inch round non-stick tins.

Place directly over a high heat for 2–3 minutes to brown the base, then bake at 200°C/400°F/gas mark 6 for about 20 minutes or until tender. Unmould.

TIMBALE DE BROCCOLI

BROCCOLI TIMBALE	This dish is shown in the photograph on page 111	Serves 10

Dry the broccoli on a kitchen cloth, then chop roughly. Reduce the cream by two-thirds, then leave to cool. Add the cream to the broccoli. Liquidise and pass through a fine sieve.

Whisk the egg and egg yolk and add

200 g/7 oz cooked broccoli
200 ml/7 fl oz double cream
1 egg
1 egg yolk
salt and freshly milled pepper

to the broccoli mixture. Season with salt and pepper.

Pour the mixture into buttered timbales and poach in a bain-Marie at 100°C/200°F/gas mark ¼ for about 35 minutes until just firm. Unmould.

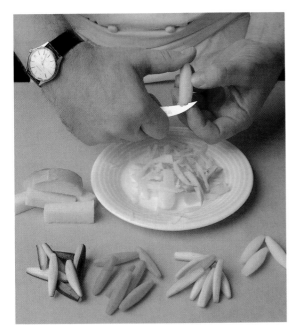

TURNING VEGETABLES

Cut the vegetables in even-sized oblongs, then
trim to elongated barrel shapes.

WILD MUSHROOMS

Scrape the stalks clean with a small knife, then
trim the bases of the stalks. Wash thoroughly
just before using. Keep small mushrooms
whole; cut larger ones in half.

PREPARING VEGETABLE 'SPAGHETTI'

The vegetables are prepared using a special
blade of a mandolin. If cutting by hand, the
vegetables should be cut in strips similar to
pasta spaghetti.

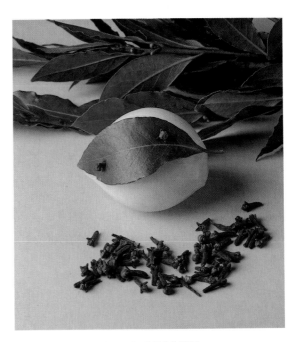

ONION PIQUE

Peel a small onion and stud it with a fresh bay
leaf and 2 whole cloves.

CREPES AUX MAIS ET POIVRONS

CORN AND PEPPER PANCAKES	This dish is shown in the photograph on page 136	*Serves 4*

Blanch the corn-on-the-cob in boiling salted water for 6 minutes and refresh. Carefully remove the corn kernels from the cob and dry them thoroughly on a kitchen cloth.

Sweat the diced red and green pepper in 15 g/½ oz of the butter in a covered pan for about 5 minutes until tender, then drain thoroughly.

Mix the cream with the flour and egg yolks, then stir in the corn and

1 corn-on-the-cob
40 g/1½ oz red pepper, finely diced
40 g/1½ oz green pepper, finely diced
40 g/1½ oz unsalted butter
100 ml/3½ fl oz double cream
25 g/1 oz plain flour
3 egg yolks
50 ml/2 fl oz oil
salt and freshly milled pepper

peppers. Season with salt and pepper.

Heat half the oil and half the remaining butter in a large frying pan. Place six metal rings about 5-cm/2-inch diameter in the pan. Fill the metal rings about 1-cm/½-inch deep with the pancake mixture. Fry until golden on one side, remove the rings, turn the pancakes and fry until golden on the other side. Repeat until all the mixture is used.

NAVETS A LA DAUPHINOISE

TURNIPS WITH CREAM	This dish is shown in the photograph on page 138	*Serves 4*

Cut the turnips in paper-thin slices, sprinkle generously with salt and leave for about 1 hour in a cool place.

Squeeze the slices of turnip in a kitchen cloth until thoroughly dry.

400 g/14 oz small turnips, peeled
200 ml/7 fl oz double cream
salt and freshly milled pepper

Season with pepper and arrange in a buttered ovenproof dish. Bring the cream to the boil and cover the turnips. Bake at 180°C/350°F/gas mark 4 for about 45 minutes until tender.

TIMBALE DE BETTERAVES

BEETROOT TIMBALE	This dish is shown in the photograph on page 74	*Serves 10*

Dry the beetroot on a kitchen cloth, then chop roughly. Mix the cream and beetroot together. Liquidise, and pass through a fine sieve.

Whisk the eggs, add to the beetroot mixture and season to taste.

150 g/5 oz cooked beetroot
100 ml/3½ fl oz double cream
2 eggs
salt and freshly milled pepper

Pour the mixture into buttered timbales (about 40-ml/1½-fl oz capacity) and poach in a bain-Marie at 100°C/200°F/gas mark ¼ for 35 minutes until just firm. Unmould.

TOMATO FILLETS

Cut plum tomatoes in quarters, cut out the seeds and carefully cut as close as possible to the skin to remove the flesh.

TOMATO ROSE

Using a serrated knife, cut a continuous spiral strip from a firm tomato, starting at the base. Keeping the skin-side outside, roll into a tight flower shape.

TURNING MUSHROOMS

1 Using a small, pointed paring knife, score the mushrooms from the centre to the edge at regular intervals, removing a narrow strip of flesh each time. Discard the stalks. 2 Turned mushrooms.

CHOU ROUGE BRAISE

BRAISED RED CABBAGE	This dish is shown in the photograph on page 150	Serves 10

1.5 kg/3 lb red cabbage, thinly sliced
200 ml/7 fl oz red wine
50 ml/2 fl oz red wine vinegar
50 g/2 oz onion, sliced
65 g/2½ oz goose fat or unsalted butter
25 g/1 oz brown sugar
400 ml/14 fl oz chicken stock (page 194)
1 clove
60 peppercorns
2 dessert apples, peeled, cored and sliced
100 g/4 oz fresh apple purée
100 ml/3½ fl oz dry white wine
salt and freshly milled pepper

Season the cabbage with salt and pepper and marinate in the red wine and red wine vinegar for 4 hours.

Sweat the onion in the goose fat until transparent, add the sugar and sweat until well glazed. Add the cabbage with its marinade and the chicken stock and transfer to an oven-proof dish. Wrap the clove and peppercorns in a piece of muslin and add to the cabbage.

Cover and braise at 170°C/325°F/gas mark 3 for 40 minutes. Stir occasionally. Add the apple slices, apple purée and white wine to the cabbage. Braise for a further 30–40 minutes or until the cabbage is tender and all the liquid has evaporated. Remove from the oven, discard the muslin bag and season to taste.

SPETZLI

EGG NOODLES WITH SPINACH	This dish is shown in the photograph on page 142	Serves 4

400 g/14 oz plain flour
6 eggs
25 g/1 oz spinach purée (page 193)
25 ml/1 fl oz oil
ground nutmeg
40 g/1½ oz unsalted butter
salt and freshly milled pepper

Mix half the flour with three of the eggs, the spinach purée, half the oil, nutmeg, salt and pepper to a very elastic dough. Beat with a wooden spoon until air bubbles develop. Mix the remaining flour, eggs and oil with the seasonings in the same way.

Bring a large saucepan of salted water with a dash of oil to the boil. Spread a small amount of either paste thinly on a thin wooden board, about 25 × 20-cm/10 × 8-inch. Dip the whole board into the boiling water and then, using palette knife, quickly scrape off small strips of the paste directly into the boiling water. Cook for about 1 minute and refresh. Repeat until both doughs are used up.

Melt the butter and toss the spetzli until warm. Season to taste.

SULFRINO BALLS

Using a sulfrino cutter, scoop small balls from firm vegetables.

VEGETABLE DIAMONDS

CABBAGE BALLS

1 Remove the outside leaves of a Savoy cabbage and discard. Cut in quarters and remove stalks. Blanch the leaves.   2 Take one or two leaves at a time and form into a ball by squeezing tightly in muslin.

POLENTA

FRIED MAIZE FLOUR DIAMONDS	This dish is shown in the photograph on page 133	*Serves 10*

Bring the water to the boil, add a pinch of salt and sprinkle in the maize flour slowly, stirring constantly. Cook over a very gentle heat for about 20 minutes, stirring frequently.

Turn the mixture on to a generously

500 ml/18 fl oz water
120 g/4½ oz fine maize flour
40 g/1½ oz unsalted butter
salt

oiled baking tray and level the surface. Cover and cool in the refrigerator for at least 2 hours.

Cut in neat diamond shapes. Melt the butter and fry the polenta diamonds until golden brown.

GNOCCHI ALLA ROMANA

FRIED SEMOLINA HALF-MOONS	This dish is shown in the the photograph on page 118	*Serves 10*

Bring the milk to the boil, then add 50 g/2 oz of the butter and a pinch of salt. Pour in the semolina, stirring constantly, and cook over a gentle heat for 15 minutes. Leave to cool slightly, then add the egg yolks and grated Parmesan. Pour the mixture on to a buttered baking tray and refrigerate

500 ml/18 fl oz milk
75 g/3 oz unsalted butter
100 g/4 oz semolina
2 egg yolks, beaten
25 g/1 oz Parmesan, grated
50 ml/2 fl oz oil
salt

for 2–3 hours until firm.

Stamp out half-moon shapes and fry in the remaining butter and oil until golden brown.

Alternatively, sprinkle with extra grated Parmesan and lightly brown under a hot grill.

TIMBALE D'ASPERGES

ASPARAGUS TIMBALE	This dish is shown in the photograph on page 60	*Serves 10*

Dry the asparagus on a kitchen cloth, then chop roughly.

Reduce the cream by two-thirds and leave to cool. Add the cream to the asparagus. Liquidise and pass through a fine sieve.

Whisk the egg and the egg yolk and

200 g/7 oz cooked asparagus trimmings
200 ml/7 fl oz double cream
1 egg
1 egg yolk
ground nutmeg
salt and freshly milled pepper

add to the asparagus mixture. Season to taste with nutmeg, salt and pepper.

Pour the mixture into buttered timbales (about 40-ml/1½-fl oz capacity) and poach in a bain-Marie at 100°C/200°F/gas mark ¼ for about 35 minutes until just firm. Unmould.

**VEGETABLE
PAYSANNE**

**VEGETABLE
JULIENNE**

**VEGETABLE
BRUNOISE**

RÖSTI DE PANAIS ET CAROTTES

PARSNIP AND CARROT RÖSTI	This dish is shown in the the photograph on page 148	Serves 4

	100 g/4 oz carrot, grated
	90 g/3½ oz unsalted butter
	100 g/4 oz parsnip, grated
	1 egg yolk
	salt and freshly milled pepper

Sweat the carrot in 20 g/¾ oz of the butter for about 2 minutes until tender. Sweat the parsnip in 20 g/¾ oz of the butter for about 6 minutes until tender.

Combine the carrot and parsnip with the egg yolk and season generously. Divide the mixture in four and shape each portion into a small, flat cake. Melt the remaining butter and fry the cakes until golden brown on both sides.

LEGUMES VARIES ROYAL

VEGETABLE MEDLEY	This dish is shown in the the photograph on page 121	Serves 4

40 g/1½ oz carrot, cooked al dente
40 g/1½ oz cauliflower, cooked al dente
40 g/1½ oz broccoli, cooked al dente
40 g/1½ oz fine green beans, cooked al dente
40 g/1½ oz courgette, cooked al dente
25 g/1 oz broad beans, cooked al dente
100 ml/3½ fl oz double cream
1 egg yolk
salt and freshly milled pepper

Cut all the vegetables except the broad beans in small cubes and season to taste. Mix the cream with the egg yolk and season generously. Stir all the vegetables into the cream mixture and use to fill four small buttered moulds or egg cups.

Cover and poach in a bain-Marie at 150°C/300°F/gas mark 2 for about 20 minutes or until just firm.

Unmould and serve with a selection of fresh vegetables.

TO CANALE

Using a canalé knife, score grooves at close,
regular intervals in the skin of vegetables such
as courgettes and cucumbers and fruit such as
lemons and oranges which gives a decorative
effect, particularly when sliced.

VEGETABLE
BATONS

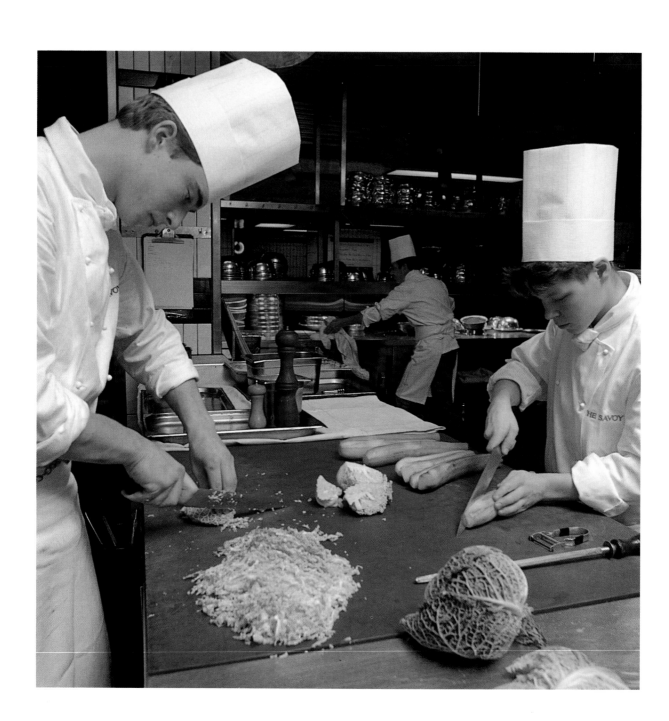

BASIC RECIPES AND PREPARATION TECHNIQUES

It is advisable to make up the basic recipes in the given quantities; any surplus can usually be refrigerated or frozen.

BECHAMEL SAUCE

40 g/1½ oz unsalted butter

50 g/2 oz plain flour

1.2 litres/2 pints milk

1 onion piqué (page 181)

salt and freshly milled pepper

Melt the butter in a saucepan, add the flour and work together to make a roux. Cook without colouring for 5–6 minutes over a gentle heat, then leave to cool. Bring the milk just to the boil with the onion piqué. Add the milk to the roux slowly, stirring all the time to avoid lumps. Cook slowly over a gentle heat for about 30 minutes. Pass through a fine sieve and season to taste.

BEEF STOCK

1 kg/2¼ lb beef bones

12 white peppercorns, crushed

1 onion, unpeeled and halved

100 g/4 oz leek, sliced

100 g/4 oz celery, sliced

½ bay leaf

1 sprig of thyme

10 g/¼ oz parsley stalks

1 clove of garlic

salt

Place the beef bones in a saucepan and just cover with cold water. Bring to the boil slowly, skimming frequently. Add the peppercorns and salt. Simmer very gently for about 2 hours. Brown the onion in a heavy-based pan. Add to the stock with the remaining ingredients. Simmer for a further hour, then pass through muslin and skim off the fat.

BEURRE BLANC

10 g/¼ oz shallot, chopped

6 white peppercorns, crushed

25 ml/1 fl oz white wine vinegar

200 ml/7 fl oz dry white wine

25 ml/1 fl oz double cream

150 g/5 oz unsalted butter, chilled and diced

cayenne

salt

Place the shallot, peppercorns, vinegar and white wine in a saucepan and reduce by half. Add the cream and reduce until the mixture thickens. Remove from the heat and work in the butter. Season with cayenne and salt and pass through a fine sieve. Keep warm in a bain-Marie.

Beurre au cerfeuil: Use herb vinegar instead of white wine vinegar. Add a few chervil stalks to the reduction. Add a sprinkling of chopped chervil to the finished sauce.

Beurre au citron: Halve the amount of vinegar and make up to 25 ml/1 fl oz with lemon juice.

Beurre au citronelle: Halve the amount of vinegar and make up to 25 ml/1 fl oz with fresh lime juice.

BLACKCURRANT SAUCE

250 g/9 oz blackcurrants

150 ml/¼ pint sugar syrup (page 204)

Purée the blackcurrants and sugar syrup in a liquidiser. Pass through a fine sieve.

PREPARING A CHICKEN SUPREME

1 Remove the 'feather' fillet from the suprême and discard the sinews. 2 Carefully cut horizontally almost through the suprême. 3 Open out flat. 4 Place both pieces of chicken between sheets of plastic and beat out flat.

CANNOISE

100 g/4 oz onion, chopped

50 g/2 oz unsalted butter

100 ml/3½ fl oz vegetable oil

1 clove of garlic, crushed

20 g/¾ oz tomato purée

150 g/5 oz plum tomato fillets, diced

100 g/4 oz red pepper, cut in small cubes

100 g/4 oz green pepper, cut in small cubes

100 g/4 oz aubergine, cut in small cubes

50 g/2 oz green courgette, cut in small cubes

50 g/2 oz yellow courgette, cut in small cubes

salt and freshly milled pepper

Sweat the onion in the butter and half the oil slowly until transparent. Add the garlic and sweat for a further 1 minute. Add the tomato purée and the tomatoes, season with salt and pepper and simmer for about 5 minutes.

Season the remaining vegetables with salt and pepper, heat the remaining oil and toss them very quickly, then add to the tomatoes. Cover and cook at 180°C/350°F/gas mark 4 for about 20 minutes. Remove from the oven and season to taste.

CARAMELISED ORANGE JULIENNE

20 g/¾ oz fine julienne of orange zest

200 ml/7 fl oz water

120 g/4½ oz caster sugar

Poach the orange julienne gently in the water until tender. Add the sugar and dissolve over a moderate heat. Bring to the boil and boil gently for 5 minutes. Leave to cool in the syrup.

Store in the syrup until required. Drain well before using.

CARROT PUREE

500 g/1 lb 2 oz carrots

40 g/1½ oz unsalted butter

salt and freshly milled pepper

Steam the carrots until tender. Purée in a food processor or liquidiser. Pass through a fine sieve, place in a saucepan and cook over a moderate heat, stirring frequently until any excess liquid has evaporated. Stir in the butter and season with salt and pepper.

Any root vegetable may be prepared in the same way.

Spinach purée: Blanch the spinach, then proceed as above.

CHICKEN ASPIC

1 pig's trotter

500 g/1 lb 2 oz chicken legs

100 g/4 oz mirepoix (page 207)

2 egg whites

1.5 litres/2½ pints chicken stock (page 194)

bouquet garni

salt and freshly milled pepper

Place the pig's trotter in cold salted water, bring to the boil, then refresh under cold, running water.

Bone out the chicken legs, chop the bones and coarsely mince the meat. Combine with the mirepoix, egg

PREPARING NOISETTES FROM A SADDLE OF LAMB

1 Pull off the skin.   2 Using a sharp knife, cut down the length of the backbone.   3 Ease the meat from the bones on either side.   4 Trim the fat and cut in noisettes about 4-cm/1½-inch thick.

whites, cold chicken stock and pig's trotter. Add the bouquet garni and salt and pepper. Bring to the boil slowly, stirring occasionally with a metal spoon. As soon as a froth forms on top of the stock, stop stirring and simmer over a very gentle heat for 1 hour. Season to taste. Pass through fine muslin, leave to cool and refrigerate until set.

The pig's trotter should release enough strength to set the aspic.

Duck aspic with port:
Prepare as above, but with duck stock (see next recipe) and duck legs. Add 100 ml/3½ fl oz of ruby port to each litre/1¾ pints of prepared aspic.

CHICKEN STOCK

| 1 boiling fowl, dressed |
| 500 g/1 lb 2 oz chicken bones (if available) |
| 12 white peppercorns, crushed |
| 1 sprig of thyme |
| a few parsley stalks |
| ½ bay leaf |
| 100 g/4 oz celery, chopped |
| 100 g/4 oz leek, chopped |
| 50 g/2 oz carrot, chopped |
| 1 small onion, unpeeled and halved |
| salt and freshly milled pepper |

Choose a saucepan not much larger than the fowl. Just cover the fowl and bones with about 1.5 litres/2½ pints cold water. Bring to the boil slowly and skim off all the fat. Add the peppercorns, herbs, celery, leek, carrot and salt. Brown the onion halves in a heavy-based pan and add to the stock. Simmer until the fowl is tender, then remove from the saucepan. Season to taste, then pass the stock through a fine sieve or muslin.

For strong chicken stock, reduce by fast boiling to half the amount.

Duck stock: Prepare as above, but with duck legs and duck bones.

CHOCOLATE SAUCE

| 100 g/4 oz cocoa powder |
| 300 ml/½ pint water |
| 225 g/8 oz caster sugar |
| 50 g/2 oz plain chocolate couverture, tempered (page 204) |

Mix the cocoa powder to a paste with a little of the water. Dissolve the sugar in the remaining water over a gentle heat. Stir in the cocoa paste and bring to the boil, stirring constantly. Remove from the heat and add the chocolate to the sauce, stirring constantly until blended. Pass through a fine sieve.

CHOUX PASTE

| 120 ml/4 fl oz milk |
| 50 g/2 oz unsalted butter |
| 65 g/2½ oz plain flour, sifted |
| 2 eggs |
| salt |

Boil the milk with the butter until the butter is melted.

PREPARING CHICKEN LEGS

1 Cut the skin around the drumstick just above the knuckle. Twist the knuckle to remove and pull away the sinews. 2 Loosen the thigh bone by easing around the flesh with a sharp knife. 3 Twist the joint and remove the bone. 4 Make an incision in the thigh skin and push the drumstick through to make a neat shape.

Reduce the heat, add the flour and salt and stir well until the mixture forms a smooth paste. Cook, stirring for 2–3 minutes. Transfer to a bowl and beat in the eggs, one at a time.

COFFEE SAUCE

10 g / ¼ oz ground coffee

500 ml / 18 fl oz vanilla sauce (page 205)

Infuse the coffee in the warm vanilla sauce for 20 minutes. Pass through a fine sieve or muslin and leave to cool.

COURT BOUILLON

100 g / 4 oz leek (white part only), thinly sliced

100 g / 4 oz celery, thinly sliced

100 g / 4 oz carrot, thinly sliced

65 g / 2½ oz button mushrooms, thinly sliced

100 g / 4 oz fennel, thinly sliced

65 g / 2½ oz shallot, finely chopped

25 g / 1 oz unsalted butter

50 ml / 2 fl oz white wine vinegar

200 ml / 7 fl oz dry white wine

2 litres / 3½ pints water

bouquet garni

½ clove of garlic

salt

Sweat the vegetables in the butter. Add the vinegar, white wine and water. Simmer for 10 minutes, then add the bouquet garni, garlic and salt. Simmer for a further 10 minutes, remove from the heat and pass through fine muslin.

CROUTONS

100 g / 4 oz white bread, cut in 5-mm / ¼-inch thick slices

100 ml / 3½ fl oz oil

50 g / 2 oz unsalted butter

Remove the crusts from the bread and cut into batons about 5-mm / ¼-inch wide and 2-cm / ¾-inch long. Heat the oil and butter together and toss the bread batons until golden brown. Drain on kitchen paper.

PREPARING SCALLOPS

1 Place the scallop rounded-side down on the work surface. Using a round-bladed knife, ease the shell all the way round. Pull hard to separate the two half shells.   2 Remove the scallop from its shell by loosening with a knife.   3 Cut around the solid white muscle and discard any membrane. Reserve the orange roe and wash thoroughly.   4 Wash and trim the scallop, then cut in half.

CUMBERLAND SAUCE

2 oranges

1 lemon

25 g / 1 oz unsalted butter

sugar

100 ml / 3½ fl oz water

10 g / ¼ oz shallot, chopped

12 peppercorns, crushed

400 ml / 14 fl oz ruby port

50 ml / 2 fl oz red wine vinegar

200 ml / 7 fl oz chicken stock (page 194)

200 g / 7 oz red currant jelly

ground ginger

Pare the rind from the oranges and lemon, blanch and refresh. Melt about one-fifth of the butter in a saucepan, add a generous pinch of sugar and caramelise lightly. Add the orange and lemon rinds and water. Reduce. Squeeze the juice from the oranges and lemon and add to the saucepan with the shallot, peppercorns, port, red wine vinegar, chicken stock, red currant jelly and a pinch of ginger. Simmer for about 10 minutes until the sauce begins to thicken slightly. Pass through a fine sieve and stir in the remaining butter.

FISH MOUSSE

500 g/1 lb 2 oz white fish fillets such as sole, monkfish, halibut, brill or pike, skinned

2 egg whites

400 ml/14 fl oz double cream

cayenne

salt and freshly milled pepper

Season the fish fillets with salt and pepper, and refrigerate for at least 1 hour. Dry the fish on a kitchen cloth and mince finely or work in a food processor until smooth. Place a fine sieve over a bowl set in ice, then pass the fish through the sieve. Add the egg whites gradually and work in thoroughly. Add the cream slowly and continue mixing over the ice until all the cream is incorporated. Season with cayenne, salt and pepper.

FISH STOCK

1 kg/2¼ lb sole or turbot bones

40 g/1½ oz shallot, chopped

20 g/¾ oz unsalted butter

200 ml/7 fl oz dry white wine

1 litre/1¾ pints water

50 g/2 oz leeks, sliced

50 g/2 oz celery, sliced

12 white peppercorns

½ bay leaf

10 g/¼ oz parsley stalks

20 g/¾ oz mushroom trimmings

salt and pepper

Chop the fish bones and wash well in cold water. Sweat the shallots in the oil, add the fish bones, cover and cook for about 3 minutes. Add the white wine, water and the remaining ingredients. Bring to the boil and simmer for about 15 minutes, skimming frequently. Pass through fine muslin and skim off any remaining fat.

FLEURONS

40 g/1½ oz puff paste (page 200)

1 egg yolk, beaten

poppy seeds

sesame seeds

Roll the puff paste 3-mm/ ⅛-inch thick, ensuring that it is rolled in different directions to prevent distortion when cooking. Using a 6-cm/2½-inch fluted cutter, stamp out four crescent-shaped pieces. Place on a buttered baking tray. Brush the tops with egg yolk and sprinkle with a few poppy and sesame seeds. Leave to rest in the refrigerator for 20 minutes. Bake at 200°C/400°F/gas mark 6 for 15 minutes until golden brown.

Other shapes such as fish or stars can be made in the same way. (See also wild mushroom fleurons, page 206.)

FRANGIPANE

120 g/4½ oz unsalted butter

120 g/4½ oz caster sugar

2 eggs, beaten

120 g/4½ oz ground almonds, sifted

25 g/1 oz plain flour, sifted

Cream the butter and sugar until pale using a mixer set on high speed. Add the eggs slowly until well incorporated. Fold in the almonds and flour.

GAME STOCK

500 g/1 lb 2 oz game trimmings and bones such as venison, pheasant or quail

20 g/¾ oz unsalted butter

120 g/4½ oz mirepoix (page 207)

200 ml/7 fl oz red wine

1.5 litres/2½ pints chicken stock (page 194)

1 bay leaf

1 sprig of thyme

12 peppercorns, crushed

salt

Roast the game trimmings and bones with the butter at 220°C/425°F/gas mark 7 for about 20 minutes until browned. Add the mirepoix and roast for a further 10 minutes. Discard the fat. Add the red wine, chicken stock, herbs and peppercorns, and simmer for about 45 minutes, skimming frequently so that the stock remains clear. Season with salt. Pass through a fine sieve or muslin.

GAZPACHO COULIS

600 g/1 lb 5 oz plum tomatoes, chopped

200 g/7 oz cucumber, peeled and seeds removed

40 g/1½ oz red pepper, chopped

40 g/1½ oz green pepper, chopped

100 g/4 oz onions, chopped

½ clove of garlic, chopped

10 g/¼ oz fresh white breadcrumbs

25 ml/1 fl oz olive oil

50 ml/2 fl oz white wine vinegar

50 ml/2 fl oz tomato ketchup

SHAPING QUENELLES

1 Using two dessertspoons or teaspoons (depending on the size required) dipped in water, take a spoonful of mousse and transfer it from one spoon to the other until a perfect quenelle is formed.   2 Place on buttered greaseproof paper.

400 ml/14 fl oz chicken stock
(page 194)

freshly chopped oregano

50 ml/2 fl oz mayonnaise
(page 199)

salt and freshly milled
pepper

Place all the vegetables in a
bowl with the breadcrumbs,
oil, vinegar, ketchup, chicken
stock, a sprinkling of oregano,
and salt and pepper. Cover
and marinate for 24 hours.

Purée in a liquidiser and stir
in the mayonnaise. Pass
through a fine sieve and
season to taste.

GENOESE SPONGE

150 ml/¼ pint beaten egg
(4–5 eggs)

120 g/4½ oz caster sugar

120 g/4½ oz plain flour,
sifted

10 g/¼ oz unsalted butter,
melted

Butter and line a 20-cm/8-
inch round cake tin. Whisk
the eggs and sugar in a bowl
over simmering water until
the mixture has increased in
volume and the whisk leaves
a trail. Fold in the flour and
melted butter. Transfer the
mixture to the prepared tin
and bake at 180°C/350°F/gas
mark 4 for about 35 minutes
until risen and firm to the
touch. Cool on a wire tray.

HOLLANDAISE
SAUCE

100 ml/3½ fl oz dry white
wine

50 ml/2 fl oz white wine
vinegar

100 ml/3½ fl oz water

12 white peppercorns,
crushed

10 g/¼ oz shallot, chopped

stalks of chervil, parsley and
tarragon

5 egg yolks

600 g/1 lb 5 oz unsalted
butter

juice of ½ lemon

salt and freshly milled
pepper

Place the white wine, vinegar,
water, peppercorns, shallot
and a few herb stalks in a
saucepan over a moderate
heat. Reduce by two-thirds
and leave to cool. Pass
through a fine sieve and add
to the egg yolks. Whisk in a
bain-Marie or over hot
water with a balloon whisk
until the mixture coats the
back of a spoon. Melt the
butter slowly and skim the
white sediment from the top.
Leave to cool to blood
temperature (36.8°C/98.4°F).
Whisk the butter slowly into
the egg mixture. Season with
lemon juice, salt and pepper.

JUS DE VEAU

5 pieces of veal bone

200 g/7 oz carrots, roughly
chopped

200 g/7 oz onions, roughly
chopped

200 g/7 oz leek, roughly
chopped

200 g/7 oz celery, roughly
chopped

1 calf's foot

1 clove of garlic, chopped

100 g/4 oz tomato purée

300 ml/½ pint white wine

10 g/¼ oz peppercorns,
crushed

a few sprigs of thyme

2 bay leaves

100 g/4 oz tomato trimmings

salt and freshly milled
pepper

Place the veal bones in a large
saucepan of cold water and
bring to the boil. Drain and
wash well under cold,
running water. Return the
bones to the pan, add half the
vegetables and cover with
cold water. Simmer for about
4 hours, then strain. Discard
the bones.

Chop the calf's foot and

roast at 220°C/425°F/gas
mark 7 until lightly browned.
Add the remaining
vegetables, garlic and tomato
purée. Roast for 15–20
minutes, stirring occasionally.
Add the white wine, prepared
stock, peppercorns, herbs and
tomato trimmings. Simmer
gently, skimming frequently.
Reduce by half and pass
through a fine sieve or
muslin. Season to taste.

Glace de viande: Reduce the
jus de veau by boiling to a
very thick, dark, syrupy glaze.

LIME SAUCE

10 g/¼ oz fine julienne of
lime zest

50 g/2 oz caster sugar

400 ml/14 fl oz water

15 g/½ oz arrowroot

500 ml/18 fl oz fresh lime
juice

Poach the lime julienne in a
little water until tender. Drain
and reserve.

Dissolve the sugar in the
water and bring to the boil.
Mix the arrowroot and lime
juice together. Stir into the
boiling liquid and cook until
thickened. Leave to cool, then
pass through a fine sieve or
muslin. Stir in the reserved
julienne.

LOBSTER MOUSSE

50 g/2 oz uncooked lobster
meat

COCKS' COMBS

Blanch by placing in cold salted water and bringing to the boil.
Drain and refresh. Place in a kitchen cloth with some coarse salt
and rub vigorously to remove the fine outer skin. Trim off the
feathery base. Cook in stock for about 30 minutes or until
tender.

½ egg white

100 ml/3½ fl oz double cream

¼ egg yolk

salt and freshly milled pepper

Dry the lobster meat thoroughly with a kitchen cloth. Season with salt and leave to rest in the refrigerator for at least 20 minutes. Dry the lobster meat again, then mince very finely or work in a food processor.

Set a small bowl in a bowl of ice. Pass the lobster through a fine sieve into the chilled bowl. Slowly add the egg white, then slowly stir in the cream, keeping the bowl over ice all the time. Add the egg yolk and season. The consistency should be almost runny at this stage. Leave to rest in the refrigerator for about 25 minutes or until the mixture becomes slightly firm.

LOBSTER SAUCE

25 ml/1 fl oz oil

500 g/1 lb 2 oz lobster shells, finely crushed (page 201)

65 g/2½ oz onions, chopped

65 g/2½ oz leek, chopped

1 clove of garlic, chopped

65 g/2½ oz plum tomato fillets, chopped

40 g/1½ oz tomato purée

200 ml/7 fl oz dry white wine

1 litre/1¾ pints chicken stock (page 194)

12 peppercorns, crushed

a few sprigs of tarragon

650 g/1 lb 7 oz unsalted butter

cayenne

salt and freshly milled pepper

Heat the oil and fry the shells quickly. Add the onion, leek, garlic, tomato and tomato purée, and fry for a further 5 minutes. Add the white wine, chicken stock, peppercorns and tarragon, and simmer for 30 minutes, skimming frequently. Pass through a fine sieve or muslin. Reduce by four-fifths. Cut the butter in small pieces and add one by one to the sauce over a gentle heat. Season with cayenne, salt and pepper.

MADEIRA SAUCE

40 g/1½ oz shallots, chopped

PRESERVING FRESH TRUFFLES

1 Scrub the truffles with a vegetable brush. 2 Place whole or thinly sliced in a preserving jar. 3 Cover with port and seal. The liquid in the jar is the truffle juice referred to in several of the recipes.

65 g/2½ oz unsalted butter

24 black peppercorns, crushed

1 sprig of thyme

50 ml/2 fl oz Madeira

50 ml/2 fl oz truffle juice (page 198)

1 litre/1¾ pints jus de veau (page 197)

Sweat the shallots in 50 g (2 oz) of the butter. Add the peppercorns, thyme, Madeira and half the truffle juice. Reduce by two-thirds and add the jus de veau. Simmer for about 10 minutes, skimming frequently. Add the remaining truffle juice and season to taste. Pass through a sieve and stir in the remaining butter.

MANGO SAUCE

3 medium-sized, ripe mangoes

juice of ½ lemon

100 ml/3½ fl oz sugar syrup (page 204)

Peel the mangoes and remove the flesh from around each stone. Liquidise to a smooth consistency. There should be about 400 ml/14 fl oz of purée. Add the lemon juice and sugar syrup. Mix thoroughly, then pass through a fine sieve or muslin.

MAYONNAISE

4 egg yolks

50 ml/2 fl oz white wine vinegar

20 g/¾ oz Dijon mustard

Worcestershire sauce

1 litre/1¾ pints vegetable oil

salt and freshly milled pepper

Combine the egg yolks, vinegar and mustard with a dash of Worcestershire sauce and salt and pepper in a food processor and mix well. Add the oil whilst the machine is working until it has all been incorporated and the mayonnaise is thick. Season to taste.

MUSHROOM DUXELLE

300 g/10 oz button mushrooms, quartered

25 g/1 oz unsalted butter

50 ml/2 fl oz dry white wine

100 ml/3½ fl oz double cream

15 g/½ oz shallot, chopped

salt and freshly milled pepper

Sweat the mushrooms in three-quarters of the butter, add the white wine and season to taste. Remove from the pan when cooked and chop very finely. Reduce the mushroom stock to a glaze, add the cream and reduce by half. Sweat the shallots in the remaining butter until transparent, add the mushrooms and cream and season to taste.

NOODLE PASTE

500 g/1 lb 2 oz plain flour

25 ml/1 fl oz oil

4 eggs

4 egg yolks

salt and freshly milled pepper

Mix all the ingredients together thoroughly until they form a smooth dough. Cover and leave to rest for at least 20 minutes in the refrigerator before using.

To prepare noodles, roll out the noodle paste as thinly as possible on a surface sprinkled with semolina. Cut into an oblong. Fold each short end in towards the centre, then fold in once more to meet in the centre. Turn the paste over and cut in very thin strips. Lift the noodles with a knife to separate them. Cook in boiling water with a dash of olive oil until al dente.

BEETROOT NOODLE PASTE

500 g/1 lb 2 oz plain flour

25 ml/1 fl oz oil

3 eggs

3 egg yolks

50 g/2 oz beetroot purée (page 193)

Proceed as above.

PREPARING OYSTERS

1 Push an oyster knife into the hinged section of the oyster.   2 Twist the knife to open the oyster.   3 Ease the knife between the oyster and the flat side of the shell to release it. Loosen the oyster from the shell. If used for cooking, remove the beard and the small, round hard muscle.

SPINACH NOODLE PASTE

500 g/1 lb 2 oz plain flour

25 ml/1 fl oz oil

3 eggs

3 egg yolks

50 g/2 oz spinach purée
(page 193)

Proceed as above.

ORANGE DRESSING

juice of 1 orange

25 ml/1 fl oz sherry vinegar

5 ml/1 teaspoon Dijon
mustard

sugar

200 ml/7 fl oz olive oil

salt and freshly milled
pepper

Reduce the orange juice by
half and leave to cool. Mix
the vinegar and mustard with
a pinch of sugar. Whisk in the
oil slowly, then whisk in the
orange juice. Season to taste.

ORANGE SAUCE

15 g/½ oz arrowroot

500 ml/18 fl oz orange juice

40 g/1½ oz caster sugar

50 ml/2 fl oz Grand Marnier

Mix the arrowroot with a
little of the cold orange juice.
Dissolve the sugar in the
remaining orange juice over a
moderate heat. Add the
arrowroot to the boiling
orange juice and stir gently
until thickened. Leave to cool,
then pass through a fine sieve
and add the Grand Marnier.

PALMIERS

200 g/7 oz puff paste (page
200)

50 ml/2 fl oz sugar syrup
(page 204)

50 g/2 oz caster sugar

Roll out the puff paste to an
oblong about 5-mm/¼-inch
thick. Brush with the sugar
syrup and sprinkle with half
the caster sugar. Fold both
short sides to meet in the
centre, then fold in half.
Leave to rest for about 20
minutes in the refrigerator.
Cut in 5-mm/¼-inch thick
slices.
    Sprinkle a buttered baking
tray with half the remaining
sugar and place the slices on
top. Sprinkle with the
remaining sugar and bake at
220°C/425°F/gas mark 7 for
about 5 minutes. Then turn
each slice over carefully and
bake for a further 5 minutes.
Cool on a wire tray.

PASTE FOR PATE EN CROUTE

200 g/7 oz plain flour

120 g/4½ oz unsalted butter,
chilled

1 egg, beaten

50 ml/2 fl oz milk

50 ml/2 fl oz water

salt

Sift the flour with a pinch of
salt. Rub in the butter until
the mixture resembles fine
crumbs. Stir in the beaten
egg, milk and water, and mix
to a smooth dough.
Refrigerate until ready to use.

PASTRY CREAM

600 ml/1 pint milk

1 vanilla pod, split

4 egg yolks

75 g/3 oz caster sugar

75 g/3 oz plain flour, sifted

Bring the milk to the boil
over a gentle heat with the
split vanilla pod. Whisk the
egg yolks and sugar together
well until pale and creamy.
Add the flour and mix to a
smooth paste. Pour on half
the boiling milk and mix well.
Return this mixture to the
saucepan with the remaining
milk, stirring constantly, and
boil for 1 minute. Pass
through a fine sieve.

PILAFF RICE

10 g/¼ oz onion, finely
chopped

50 ml/2 fl oz oil

200 g/7 oz Patna rice

500 ml/18 fl oz vegetable
stock (page 206)

1 bay leaf

salt and freshly milled
pepper

Sweat the onion in the oil
until transparent. Add the rice
and stir until it is completely
coated with oil. Add the
boiling vegetable stock and
the bay leaf. Season with salt
and pepper. Cover and cook
at 180°C/350°F/gas mark 4
for 20 minutes, or until
tender.

Saffron rice: Add a pinch of
saffron strands with the stock.

PUFF PASTE

675 g/1½ lb unsalted butter

675 g/1½ lb plain flour

5–7.5 ml/1–1½ teaspoons
salt

275 ml/9 fl oz water, chilled

juice of ½ lemon

Work together 500 g/1 lb 2 oz
of the butter with 175 g/6 oz
of the flour on a cool surface.
When well mixed, form into a
12.5-cm/5-inch block, 4-cm/
1½-inch deep and refrigerate.
    Rub the remaining butter
into the remaining flour with
the salt until the mixture
resembles fine breadcrumbs.
Add the chilled water and
lemon juice to form a dough,
mix until smooth and elastic.
    Shape the dough into a
small ball, then make two
incisions to one-third of the
depth to form a cross.
    Open out the points and
roll out each one to about
5-mm/¼-inch thickness,
12.5-cm/5-inch wide and
12.5-cm/5-inch long. Place
the butter and flour block in

USING A TRELLIS CUTTER

1 Roll out the paste thinly and cut into an oblong. Roll the
trellis cutter along the length of the paste.   2 Carefully ease
open to give a lattice effect.

1

2

the centre of the dough and fold the flaps over anti-clockwise, ensuring that the edges are well sealed. Roll the dough into a 30 × 60-cm/ 12 × 24-inch oblong. Fold the short sides to meet in the middle, then fold in half to form four equal layers; this is called a double-turn. Cover with a damp cloth and leave to rest in the refrigerator for at least 30 minutes. Repeat the process four times, then leave the dough, covered, in the refrigerator to rest, preferably overnight.

RASPBERRY SAUCE

300 g/10 oz raspberries

10 ml/2 teaspoons lemon juice

40 g/1½ oz icing sugar

Purée the raspberries in a liquidiser, then add the lemon juice and icing sugar. Pass through a fine sieve or muslin.

SALAD DRESSING

50 g/2 oz Dijon mustard

150 ml/¼ pint white wine vinegar

800 ml/27 fl oz olive oil

caster sugar

salt and freshly milled pepper

Mix the mustard and vinegar together. Add the oil, stirring constantly. Season with sugar, salt and pepper.

SAVOY DRESSING

40 ml/1½ fl oz red wine vinegar

10 g/¼ oz Dijon mustard

½ clove of garlic, crushed

40 ml/1½ fl oz sugar syrup (page 204)

Worcestershire sauce

Tabasco

50 ml/2 fl oz olive oil

25 ml/1 fl oz soy sauce

25 ml/1 fl oz tomato ketchup

40 g/1½ oz leek and carrot, cut in brunoise and blanched

salt and freshly milled pepper

Whisk the vinegar, mustard, garlic and sugar syrup together. Add Worcestershire sauce, Tabasco, salt and pepper to taste. Gradually whisk in the olive oil, soy sauce and tomato ketchup. Season to taste and stir in the vegetable brunoise.

SHORT PASTE

50 g/1¾ oz unsalted butter, cut in small dice

50 g/1¾ oz lard, cut in small dice

200 g/7 oz plain flour

35 ml/7 teaspoons water

salt

Rub the butter and lard into the flour with a pinch of salt until the mixture resembles fine breadcrumbs. Add the water and quickly mix to a smooth dough. It is important to avoid over-mixing as this will produce a tough pastry. Cover and leave to rest in the refrigerator.

STRAWBERRY SAUCE

400 g/14 oz strawberries

50 g/2 oz icing sugar

Purée the strawberries and sugar in a liquidiser. Pass through a fine sieve.

STRAWBERRY SORBET

250 g/9 oz strawberries

150 ml/¼ pint water

100 g/4 oz caster sugar

10 ml/2 teaspoons lemon juice

Purée all the ingredients in a liquidiser. Pass through a fine sieve or muslin. Freeze in a sorbetière.

Alternatively, freeze in a rigid container, then work in a food processor.

STUFFING FOR QUAIL

50 g/2 oz chicken livers

100 ml/3½ fl oz milk

10 g/¼ oz shallot, chopped

50 g/2 oz unsalted butter

1 dessert apple, peeled, cored and sliced

10 g/¼ oz dried morels, soaked in cold water for at least 1 hour

25 g/1 oz lean pork, cut in cubes

20 g/¾ oz belly of pork, cut in cubes

50 g/2 oz veal, cut in cubes

½ egg, beaten

25 ml/1 fl oz Madeira

salt and freshly milled pepper

Marinate the chicken livers in the milk overnight, then wash and dry.

Sweat the shallots in half the butter until transparent. Add the apple slices. Drain and dry the morels, then sweat in the remaining butter, season to taste and leave to cool. Finely mince the lean pork, belly of pork and veal twice or finely chop in a food processor. Mince the apple and shallot mixture and the chicken livers. Add to the minced meats, mix well and mix in the egg. Reduce the Madeira, add to the mixture. Pass through a fine sieve. Season generously.

CRUSHING SHELLS

1 Place the shells in a large bowl.   2 Crush with the end of a rolling pin until quite fine. Small quantities may be crushed in a pestle and mortar.

REMOVING THE SHELL FROM A LOBSTER

1 Twist off the two large claws.   2 Twist the head to separate it from the tail.   3 Lay the tail on its side and press firmly to crack the undershell.   4 Carefully peel away the shell.   5 Twist the large claws at the first joint to separate them from the knuckle.   6 Tap both ends on the work surface to loosen the flesh.   7 Break off the small pincer claw and ease out the flesh.   8 Using a sharp knife, carefully cut away the side of the shell, then crack the claw round the centre and carefully pull apart to release the flesh.   9 Cut the lobster tail in angled slices.   10 The prepared lobster.

PREPARING ORANGE SEGMENTS

1 Using a serrated knife, cut off the top and base of the orange, then work down the side removing the skin and pith in sections.   2 Carefully ease the segments from the membrane.

SUGAR SYRUP

500 g / 1 lb 2 oz caster sugar

1 litre / 1¾ pints water

50 ml / 2 fl oz lemon juice

Dissolve the sugar in the water over a moderate heat. Add the lemon juice and bring to the boil. Leave to cool, strain and use as required.

SWEET PASTE

225 g / 8 oz unsalted butter

100 g / 4 oz caster sugar

1 egg, beaten

350 g / 12 oz plain flour

salt

Cream the butter and sugar together until very pale. Slowly beat in the egg. Slowly add the flour with a pinch of salt and mix to a smooth paste. Cover and leave to rest in the refrigerator for at least 1 hour.

TEMPERING CHOCOLATE

Cut the required amount of chocolate couverture in small pieces. Melt in a bain-Marie over a very low heat. Do not allow the water to become too hot as any steam would spoil the chocolate. (Water is couverture's worst enemy.) Heat the chocolate to 50°C / 122°F.

Cool the chocolate in a bain-Marie containing cold water. Using a plastic spatula, scrape the cooling chocolate from the edges and bottom of the bowl and stir constantly to ensure the chocolate remains smooth. Reduce the temperature of the chocolate to 28°C / 82°F. At this temperature the chocolate

should be thickening.

Raise the temperature to 30°C / 86°F in a bain-Marie containing warm water. At this stage of preparation the temperature should not exceed 30°C / 86°F. If it does, the chocolate should be cooled again to 28°C / 82°F and brought back slowly to 30°C / 86°F. At 30°C / 86°F the chocolate should be smooth, slightly thickened but still pourable.

Before using the chocolate, test it by dipping the end of a palette knife into the chocolate and refrigerating until set. Touch the chocolate lightly with your thumb. If the chocolate melts immediately, it has not been correctly tempered and the process must be repeated.

REMOVING THE TAIL SHELL FROM LANGOUSTINE AND CRAYFISH

1 Using scissors, make an incision in the under-surface, starting at the tail. 2 Cut along the length of the tail on both sides and carefully peel back the shell. 3 Using a cocktail stick, loosen the tail meat.

TOMATO COULIS

40 g / 1½ oz onion, finely chopped

1 clove of garlic, chopped

65 g / 2½ oz unsalted butter

400 g / 14 oz plum tomatoes, quartered

40 g / 1½ oz tomato purée

6 basil leaves with stalks

100 ml / 3½ fl oz vegetable stock (page 206)

salt and freshly milled pepper

Sweat the onion and garlic in 20 g / ¾ oz of the butter until transparent. Add the tomatoes and tomato purée with the basil stalks and vegetable stock and simmer gently for about 20 minutes until the tomatoes are thoroughly cooked. Pass through a fine sieve. Return to the heat and reduce to the desired consistency. Season to taste, add the chopped basil leaves and stir in the remaining butter.

TUILE MIXTURE

100 g/4 oz plain flour

100 g/4 oz icing sugar

100 g/4 oz unsalted butter, melted

2 egg whites

Sift the flour and icing sugar into a mixing bowl. Quickly stir in the melted butter and egg whites to make a smooth paste. Refrigerate for 30 minutes.

Spread the mixture into a stencil to form the desired shape, such as a tulip (see Tulipe de Sorbet aux Fruits d'Eté, page 172).

VANILLA ICE CREAM

25 g/1 oz milk powder

500 ml/18 fl oz milk

300 ml/½ pint double cream

1 vanilla pod, split

5 egg yolks

100 g/4 oz caster sugar

Mix the milk powder to a thick paste with a little of the milk. Stir in the remaining milk. Add the milk to the cream and bring to the boil with the split vanilla pod. Allow to infuse for 15 minutes. Whisk the egg yolks and sugar together, pour the infused milk on top and mix well.

Transfer the mixture to a clean saucepan and cook over a very gentle heat, stirring all the time with a wooden spoon until the sauce becomes thick and coats the back of the spoon. It is important not to boil the mixture at this stage – otherwise it will separate. Cool and pass through a fine sieve.

Freeze in an ice cream machine to a light consistency. Store in the freezer for 2 hours until firm and ready to scoop.

Alternatively, freeze in a rigid container until ice crystals begin to form. Beat well or work in a food processor until smooth. Freeze for at least 4 hours or until required.

VANILLA SAUCE

500 ml/18 fl oz milk

1 vanilla pod

6 egg yolks

75 g/3 oz caster sugar

Heat the milk and infuse the vanilla pod in it for about 10 minutes. Whisk the egg yolks and sugar together. Bring the milk to the boil, pour on to the egg yolk mixture and mix thoroughly. Place the mixture in a clean pan and stir gently with a wooden spoon over a low heat until the sauce thickens and coats the back of the spoon. Leave to cool, then pass through a fine sieve.

VANILLA SPONGE SHEET

600 ml/1 pint beaten egg

50 ml/2 fl oz egg yolk

400 g/14 oz caster sugar

250 g/9 oz plain flour, sifted

Butter and line two large baking trays. Whisk the beaten egg and yolks with the sugar in a mixer set at high speed for 7 minutes, then at slow speed for 3 minutes. Fold in the flour. Spread a thin layer of the mixture on to the prepared trays and bake immediately at 230°C/450°F/gas mark 8 for about 5 minutes. Leave to cool on the tray, then gently peel off the lining paper.

BONING OUT A DUCK

1 Remove the wish-bone. 2 Using a filleting knife and starting at the head end, work as closely as possible to the carcass, easing the flesh from the bone to remove it completely. Take care not to pierce the skin. 3 Bone out the legs and wings in a similar way.

VEAL MOUSSE

100 g/4 oz very lean veal

1 egg white

200 ml/7 fl oz double cream

salt and freshly milled pepper

Finely mince the veal or chop very finely in a food processor. Position a fine sieve over a bowl set in ice. Pass the veal through the sieve. Add the egg white and stir in thoroughly, with the bowl still set over the ice, until the mixture feels very stiff. Add the cream slowly, stirring constantly. Season generously with salt and pepper.

Chicken mousse: Use lean chicken meat to replace the veal.

VEGETABLE STOCK

50 g/2 oz shallots, chopped

50 g/2 oz unsalted butter

300 g/10 oz carrots, sliced

200 g/7 oz leek, sliced

200 g/7 oz fennel, sliced

200 g/7 oz celery, sliced

200 g/7 oz celeriac, sliced

200 ml/7 fl oz dry white wine

24 white peppercorns, crushed

1.5 litres/2½ pints chicken stock (page 194)

salt and freshly milled pepper

Sweat the shallots in the butter, then add all the remaining vegetables. Sweat for about 6 minutes in a covered pan. Season with salt and pepper and add the white wine, peppercorns and chicken stock. Simmer for about 30 minutes, then pass through a fine sieve or muslin.

WHITE WINE SAUCE

10 g/¼ oz shallot, chopped

12 white peppercorns, crushed

100 ml/3½ fl oz dry white wine

200 ml/7 fl oz fish stock (page 196)

100 ml/3½ fl oz vegetable stock (page 206)

100 ml/3½ fl oz double cream

cayenne

salt

Place the shallot, peppercorns and white wine in a saucepan and reduce by two-thirds. Add the fish and vegetable stocks and reduce again by two-thirds. Add the double cream and reduce by half. Season to taste with the cayenne and salt.

WILD MUSHROOM FLEURONS

10 g/¼ oz shallot, finely chopped

20 g/¾ oz unsalted butter

40 g/1½ oz assorted wild mushrooms, cleaned

25 ml/1 fl oz ruby port

25 ml/1 fl oz truffle juice (page 198)

40 g/1½ oz puff paste (page 200)

1 egg yolk

salt and freshly milled pepper

JOINTING A CHICKEN

1 Remove the legs. 2 Cut through the skin where the wing and breast join and scrape the meat from the wing bone. 3 Separate at the first joint. 4 Remove the wishbone. Remove the skin from the breast, if necessary, and carefully remove the breast from the carcass.

DRYING LOBSTER EGGS

Hold the live lobster firmly in one hand and using a spoon, scrape the eggs from the under-surface around the tail fins. Blanch the eggs in boiling salted water, drain and refresh, then dry thoroughly. Place on a dish and leave in the oven at lowest setting until dried.

Sweat the shallot in the butter until transparent.

Cut the wild mushrooms in 5-mm/¼-inch cubes, add to the shallots and sweat for a further 5 minutes. Season with salt and pepper and remove from the saucepan. Add the port and truffle juice to the saucepan and reduce.

Stir in the mushrooms. Season to taste and leave to cool.

Roll out the puff paste about 3-mm/⅛-inch thick and stamp out twenty 4-cm/

1½-inch rounds. Brush the edges with egg yolk. Divide the mushroom mixture between half the puff paste rounds and cover with the remaining rounds. Seal the edges well. Brush with egg yolk and leave to rest for about 20 minutes. Bake at 200°C/400°F/gas mark 6 for 15 minutes until golden.

GLOSSARY

BREAD FLUTE

A thin French bread stick similar to a baguette.

CULINARY TERMS

Al dente: Usually applied to vegetables and pasta which are slightly undercooked and so remain crisp.

Blanch: Usually a preliminary stage of cooking. Plunge food in cold or boiling water, bring quickly to the boil and cook for a short time. Drain and refresh to prevent further cooking. Vegetables are usually blanched in boiling water to retain their colour, meat and bones in cold water. Food can also be blanched without colouring by plunging in moderately hot oil.

Deglaze: To dilute the concentrated juices in a saucepan or roasting tin in which meat, poultry, game or fish has been fried, braised or roasted. Wine, fortified wine or stock are usually used for this purpose.

Reduce: To reduce the volume of a liquid by evaporation by boiling in an uncovered saucepan. Used to thicken a sauce and concentrate the flavour.

Refresh: To plunge in iced water until cold. Used to retain the colour of vegetables or to halt the cooking process.

Sweat: To cook food, usually vegetables, very gently in a mixture of butter and oil without colouring until tender.

EGG FILLETS

Shell a hard-boiled egg and using a potato peeler, peel off thin strips. Cut as required.

GRIOTTINE CHERRIES

Wild morello cherries commercially preserved in a light brandy syrup.

HERBS (deep-fried)

Wash and thoroughly dry fresh herbs or leaves such as parsley, sage, basil, rosemary or celery. Dip in very hot oil for 2 seconds and remove. Drain on a kitchen cloth.

LEAF GELATINE

Soak leaves of gelatine in cold water for about 15 minutes to soften. Drain and dissolve in stock or sugar syrup over a gentle heat.

MIREPOIX

A mixture of finely diced vegetables to include equal quantities of leek, celery, carrot and onion, flavoured with a few peppercorns, a bay leaf and a sprig of thyme.

White mirepoix: A mixture of the white part of a leek, celery and onion, flavoured as above.

PISTACHIOS AND WALNUTS (to remove skins)

Just cover the nuts with milk and bring to the boil. Remove the skin whilst warm.

QUAILS' EGGS

For soft-boiled eggs, cook in boiling salted water for 2 minutes. Drain, refresh and peel.

REINETTE APPLE

A small French red dessert apple available from September to February.

SHELLFISH (to cook)

Lobster: Plunge a 450 g/1 lb live lobster into boiling salted water and cook for 5 or 10 minutes, drain and refresh. Cook for 5 minutes if it is to be reheated in the recipe, for 10 minutes if it is served cold.

Crayfish: Cook in the same way for 2 minutes.

Langoustine: Cook in the same way for 3 minutes.

SNAILS

Good quality fresh snails are only available in the spring so use canned ones as an alternative.

SWEETBREADS

Place in cold salted water for about 2 hours to remove any blood, changing the water frequently. Place in a saucepan of cold water, bring to the boil, drain and refresh. Simmer in salted water with 1 onion piqué (page 181) for 40 minutes. Cool in the water. Remove the skin and membrane, and dry thoroughly.

COCKTAILS

Left to right TIP OF THE TONGUE; SAVOY AFFAIR

COCKTAILS

CHAMPAGNE COCKTAILS

CHAMPAGNE COCKTAIL

Put 1 lump of sugar into a champagne glass and saturate it with Angostura bitters. Fill the glass with cold Champagne and serve with a slice of orange. Add a teaspoonful of brandy if desired.

FRAISE ROYALE

Crush 2 strawberries and top up with Champagne.

LADY OF MEY

Created in honour of the Queen Mother's 80th birthday.

1 fl oz passion fruit juice

½ fl oz Cherry Heering

½ fl oz brandy

Shake and top up with Champagne.

MOONWALK

Created in honour of the intrepid astronauts.

1 fl oz Grand Marnier

1 fl oz fresh grapefruit juice

2 dashes of orange flower water

Shake and pour into a champagne glass. Top up with Champagne.

PECHE ROYALE

Crush half a peach and top up with Champagne.

ROYAL SILVER

Created in 1977 to celebrate the Silver Jubilee of the Queen.

½ fl oz Cointreau

½ fl oz Poire William

1 fl oz fresh grapefruit juice

Top up with Champagne.

SAVOY AFFAIR

¼ fl oz fresh lime juice

¼ fl oz passion fruit juice

¼ fl oz Fraise de Bordeaux

¼ fl oz peach liqueur

Frost the rim of a glass with sugar. Shake the ingredients and top up with Champagne. Decorate with a sugar-frosted strawberry.

SAVOY 90

Created in 1979 in celebration of the Savoy's 90th anniversary.

¾ fl oz Amaretto

¼ fl oz fresh lime juice

Top up with Champagne.

SAVOY ROYALE

Crush 2 strawberries and half a peach and top up with Champagne.

SAVOY SPRINGTIME

¼ fl oz gin

¼ fl oz Cointreau

¼ fl oz fresh orange juice

Shake, add a dash of fresh orange juice and top up with Champagne.

SUPER SAVOY

One of three cocktails created for British Airways when Concorde was launched.

½ Cointreau

¼ fresh orange juice

¼ Campari

Top up with Champagne.

TIP OF THE TONGUE

⅓ fl oz Medori

⅓ fl oz passion fruit juice

⅓ fl oz gin

dash of egg white

dash of syrup

Shake and strain into a glass. Top up with Champagne.

COCKTAILS

ALLIES COCKTAIL

Dating back to World War II when the American Bar was a favourite haunt of war correspondents.

½ dry gin

½ dry vermouth

2 dashes of Kummel

Shake well and strain into a cocktail glass.

AMERICAN COCKTAIL

⅓ Campari

⅔ sweet vermouth

cube of ice

Use a wine glass. Fill with soda water, stir and add a twist of lemon peel.

Left to right   MARGARET ROSE; DRY MARTINI; SEA BREEZE; FALLEN ANGEL; FROZEN DAIQUIRI

ANGEL FACE

⅓ dry gin

⅓ apricot brandy

⅓ apple brandy

Shake well and strain into a cocktail glass.

BETWEEN-THE-SHEETS COCKTAIL

1 dash of fresh lemon juice

⅓ brandy

⅓ Cointreau

⅓ Bacardi rum

Shake well and strain into a cocktail glass.

BLOODY MARY COCKTAIL

1½ fl oz vodka

2 fl oz tomato juice

½ fl oz fresh lemon juice

2 dashes of Worcestershire sauce

Shake and strain into a medium-sized wine glass.

BLUE HAWAIIAN

1 fl oz white rum

½ fl oz blue Curaçao

2 fl oz fresh pineapple juice

1 fl oz coconut cream

crushed ice

Blend and pour into a tall glass. Decorate with a slice of orange, a slice of lime and a maraschino cherry.

BULLSHOT COCKTAIL

1 fl oz vodka

4 fl oz beef bouillon or condensed consommé

1 dash of fresh lemon juice

2 dashes of Worcestershire sauce

celery salt

Shake and strain into a large glass.

CARUSO COCKTAIL

⅓ dry gin

⅓ dry vermouth

⅓ green Crème de Menthe

Shake well and strain into a cocktail glass.

DAIQUIRI COCKTAIL

1 teaspoon powdered sugar

¼ fresh lime juice

¾ Bacardi rum

Shake well and strain into a cocktail glass.

DEBUTANTE COCKTAIL

The name of this cocktail evokes memories of a vanished era when the London Season was strictly observed by both the aristocracy and those with social aspirations.

⅓ gin

⅓ fresh lemon juice

⅙ Crème de Noyaux

⅙ fresh lime juice

1 egg white

Shake and strain into a cocktail glass.

DRY MARTINI COCKTAIL

⅕ dry vermouth

⅘ dry gin

Stir well with ice and serve with a squeeze of lemon rind.

FALLEN ANGEL COCKTAIL

1 dash of Angostura bitters

2 dashes of green Crème de Menthe

juice of 1 lemon or ½ lime

2 fl oz dry gin

Shake well and strain into a cocktail glass. Decorate with a green maraschino cherry.

FROZEN DAIQURI

juice of ½ lime

1 teaspoon powdered sugar

2 fl oz Bacardi rum

1 dash of Maraschino

Put into an electric mixer with crushed ice and pour unstrained into a champagne glass. Add a maraschino cherry and serve with straws.

GREEN-EYED MONSTER

⅓ dry gin

⅓ sweet vermouth

⅓ green Chartreuse

Stir with ice and strain into a cocktail glass.

HARVEY WALLBANGER

1½ fl oz vodka

4 fl oz fresh orange juice

2 teaspoons Galliano

Build into an ice-filled highball glass. Serve with straws.

INK STREET COCKTAIL

Ink Street represents Fleet Street, for many years the heart (*sic*) of newspaper publishing.

⅓ rye whisky

⅓ fresh orange juice

⅓ fresh lemon juice

Shake well and strain into a cocktail glass.

IOLANTHE COCKTAIL

Appropriately named after one of Gilbert and Sullivan's most popular operas, first performed at the Savoy Theatre.

⅓ brandy

⅓ Lillet

⅙ Grand Marnier

⅙ fresh orange juice

3 dashes of orange bitters

Shake and strain into a cocktail glass.

Left to right   MAI TAI; WHITE LADY; TEQUILA SUNRISE; BLUE HAWAIIAN

LEAP YEAR COCKTAIL

Created by Harry Craddock for the Leap Year celebrations at the Savoy on 29 February 1928, this cocktail is reputed to have been responsible for more proposals than any other that has ever been mixed!

1 dash of fresh lemon juice
2/3 gin
1/6 Grand Marnier
1/6 sweet vermouth

Shake well and serve in a cocktail glass. Squeeze lemon peel on top.

MAGGIE BLUE

Created in honour of Margaret Thatcher's triumphant success in the General Election of 1979.

1/2 fl oz vodka
1/4 fl oz Framboise
3/4 fl oz fresh lime juice
1 dash of gomme syrup
1 dash of blue Curaçao

Shake and serve in a cocktail glass.

MAI TAI COCKTAIL

1 fl oz light rum
1 fl oz golden rum
1/2 fl oz Curaçao
juice of 1 lime
1 fl oz fresh pineapple juice
3 dashes of gomme syrup
1 dash of Grenadine

Shake and pour into a large old-fashioned glass filled with ice. Decorate with a piece of pineapple, a maraschino cherry and a sprig of mint.

MANHATTAN COCKTAIL

1 dash of Angostura bitters
2/3 rye whisky
1/3 sweet vermouth

Stir well and strain into a cocktail glass. Serve with a maraschino cherry.

MARGARET ROSE COCKTAIL

Named after Princess Margaret who was always called Margaret Rose as a little girl.

1/3 dry gin
1/3 Calvados
1/6 Cointreau
1/6 fresh lemon juice
1 dash of Grenadine

Shake well and strain into a cocktail glass.

MERRY WIDOW COCKTAIL

2 dashes of Pernod
2 dashes of Angostura bitters
2 dashes of Bénédictine
1/2 dry vermouth
1/2 dry gin

Stir well and strain into a cocktail glass. Twist lemon peel on top. The original version of this cocktail contained absinthe but Pernod is now used.

MIKADO COCKTAIL

Another cocktail emphasising the D'Oyly Carte connection.

2 dashes of Angostura bitters
2 dashes of Crème de Noyau
2 dashes of Orgeat syrup
2 dashes of Curaçao
1 fl oz brandy

Shake well and strain into a cocktail glass.

MILLION DOLLAR COCKTAIL

One of the cocktails included in the first edition of *The Savoy Cocktail Book* when a million dollars represented a fortune.

1 tablespoon fresh pineapple juice
1 teaspoon Grenadine
1 egg white
1/3 sweet vermouth
2/3 gin

Shake well and strain into a medium-sized glass.

OLD FASHIONED COCKTAIL

1 lump of sugar
2 dashes of Angostura bitters
2 fl oz rye whisky

Crush the sugar and bitters together in a medium-sized glass. Add the whisky and a cube of ice and decorate with a twist of lemon peel, a slice of orange and a maraschino cherry. This cocktail can be made with other spirits if liked.

PINA COLADA

1 fl oz white rum
1 fl oz dark rum
2 fl oz fresh pineapple juice
1 fl oz coconut cream
1 dash of fresh lime juice
crushed ice

Blend and pour into a tall glass. Decorate with a slice of lime, a piece of pineapple and a maraschino cherry. Serve with straws.

ROB ROY COCKTAIL

1 dash of Angostura bitters
1/3 sweet vermouth
2/3 Scotch whisky

Stir well and strain into a cocktail glass.

ROLLS-ROYCE COCKTAIL

1/3 brandy
1/3 Cointreau
1/3 fresh orange juice

Shake well and strain into a cocktail glass.

SCREWDRIVER COCKTAIL

1/3 vodka
2/3 fresh orange juice

Shake well and strain into a long glass. Add ice and a slice of orange.

Left to right GOLDEN CADILLAC; GRASSHOPPER; UNION JACK; WHITE RUSSIAN

SEA-BREEZE

½ vodka

⅙ dry vermouth

⅙ blue Curaçao

⅙ Galliano

Stir and strain into an ice-filled old-fashioned glass. Decorate with a slice of orange.

SIDECAR

¼ fresh lemon juice

¼ Cointreau

½ brandy

Shake well and strain into a cocktail glass.

TANGO COCKTAIL

Named after the dance beloved by the Bright Young Things, as they were popularly known, who found the music of the Savoy Orpheans irresistible.

2 dashes of Curaçao

juice of ¼ orange

¼ dry vermouth

¼ sweet vermouth

½ dry gin

Shake well and strain into a cocktail glass.

TEQUILA SUNRISE

1 fl oz Tequila

4 fl oz fresh orange juice

2 dashes of Grenadine

Build the Tequila and orange juice in an ice-filled old-fashioned glass and stir. Add the Grenadine and decorate with a slice of orange.

TRILBY COCKTAIL

2 dashes of Pernod

2 dashes of orange bitters

⅓ Parfait Amour

⅓ Scotch whisky

⅓ sweet vermouth

Shake well and strain into a cocktail glass. The original version of this cocktail contained absinthe but Pernod is now used.

TOM AND JERRY COCKTAIL

If not a classic cocktail, this is a veteran which was served in the taprooms of the United States in the nineteenth century.

1 egg

1 fl oz rum

1 fl oz brandy

1 tablespoon powdered sugar

Beat the yolk and white of the egg separately, then mix together. Use a stem glass or a china mug; add the spirits and sugar, fill up with boiling water and grate nutmeg on top.

WHITE LADY

¼ fresh lemon juice

¼ Cointreau

½ dry gin

Shake well and strain into a cocktail glass, in which a maraschino cherry has been placed.

AFTER-DINNER COCKTAILS

BLACK RUSSIAN

⅔ vodka

⅓ Kahlúa

Build in an ice-filled old-fashioned glass.

BRANDY ALEXANDER

⅓ Crème de Cacao

⅓ brandy

⅓ double cream

Shake well and strain into a cocktail glass.

GODFATHER

1½ fl oz vodka

¾ fl oz Amaretto

Build in an ice-filled old-fashioned glass.

GOLDEN CADILLAC

1 fl oz Galliano

1 fl oz white Crème de Cacao

1 fl oz double cream

Shake and strain into a cocktail glass.

GRASSHOPPER

⅓ white Crème de Cacao

⅓ green Crème de Menthe

⅓ double cream

Shake and strain into a cocktail glass.

RUSTY NAIL

½ Scotch whisky

½ Drambuie

Stir well and strain into a cocktail glass. This cocktail can also be served on the rocks.

SAVOY COCKTAIL

⅓ Crème de Cacao

⅓ Bénédictine

⅓ brandy

Use a liqueur glass and pour the ingredients carefully so that they do not mix.

STINGER

¼ white Crème de Menthe

¾ brandy

Shake well and strain into a cocktail glass.

UNION JACK

⅓ Grenadine

⅓ Maraschino

⅓ green Chartreuse

Use a liqueur glass and pour the ingredients carefully so that they do not mix.

WHITE RUSSIAN

⅓ vodka

⅓ Kahlúa

⅓ double cream

Build in an ice-filled old-fashioned glass.

Left to right GRAND ROYAL; PLANTER'S PUNCH; GIN DAISY; MOSCOW MULE; BRANDY FIX

NON-ALCOHOLIC COCKTAILS

LONG BOAT COCKTAIL

2 fl oz lime juice cordial
2 cubes of ice

Serve in a long tumbler, topped up with ginger beer. Decorate with a sprig of fresh mint.

PUSSY FOOT COCKTAIL

⅓ fresh orange juice
⅓ fresh lemon juice
⅓ fresh lime juice
dash of Grenadine
1 egg yolk

Shake and strain into a medium-sized glass. Add a maraschino cherry, a slice of orange and a splash of soda water.

TONGA COCKTAIL

½ fresh lemon juice
½ fresh pineapple juice
1 teaspoon Grenadine
1 egg white

Shake well and pour into a long-stemmed glass. Add a cube of ice and fill with lemonade. Decorate with a maraschino cherry and a slice of orange.

COOLERS

APRICOT COOLER

juice of ½ lemon or 1 lime
2 dashes of Grenadine
1 fl oz apricot brandy

Shake well, strain into a long tumbler and fill with soda water.

MOSCOW MULE

2 fl oz vodka
1 dash of fresh lime juice
2 cubes of ice

Serve in a long tumbler and fill with ginger beer. Decorate with a slice of lime and a sprig of fresh mint.

PLANTER'S PUNCH

1 fl oz fresh lemon or lime juice
½ fl oz gomme syrup
1 dash of Angostura bitters
2 fl oz Jamaica rum

Shake; pour unstrained into a long tumbler, add a slice of pineapple, a slice of orange and a maraschino cherry. Serve with straws.

TOM COLLINS

juice of ½ lemon
1½ teaspoons powdered sugar
2 fl oz dry gin

Shake well and strain into a long tumbler. Add a cube of ice and top up with soda water.

DAISIES

GIN DAISY

juice of ½ lemon
¾ teaspoon powdered sugar
6 dashes of Grenadine
2 fl oz gin

Use a long tumbler. Half fill with cracked ice and stir until the glass is frosted. Fill with soda water, put 4 sprigs of fresh green mint on top and decorate with slices of fruit.

WHISKY DAISY

3 dashes of gomme syrup
juice of ½ small lemon
2 fl oz bourbon or rye whisky

Fill a cocktail shaker one-third full with shaved ice. Shake thoroughly, strain into a small tumbler and fill up with sparkling mineral water.

FIXES

In making Fixes be careful to put the lemon rind in the glass.

BRANDY FIX

1 teaspoon sugar dissolved in 1 teaspoon water
juice of ½ lemon
½ fl oz cherry brandy
1 fl oz brandy

Frost the rim of a small tumbler with sugar. Pour the ingredients into the glass and fill with fine ice. Stir slowly. Decorate with a slice of orange and a maraschino cherry. Serve with straws.

SANTA CRUZ FIX

1 tablespoon sugar
¼ lemon
1 fl oz water
2 fl oz rum

Pour into a small tumbler and fill two-thirds full with shaved ice. Stir with a spoon and decorate with fresh fruit.

FIZZES

BUCKS FIZZ

Put ½ fl oz fresh orange juice in a wine glass and fill with Champagne.

DERBY FIZZ

Named after the world-famous race run at Epsom in early summer and traditionally celebrated at the Savoy with lavish parties.

5 dashes of fresh lemon juice
1 teaspoon powdered sugar
1 egg
2 fl oz rye or Scotch whisky
3 dashes of Curaçao

Shake well, strain into a medium-sized glass and fill with soda water.

Left to right EGG SOUR; HORSE'S NECK; PINEAPPLE JULEP; SAVOY RICKEY; SINGAPORE SLING

GRAND ROYAL FIZZ

juice of ½ lemon

1½ teaspoons powdered sugar

2 fl oz gin

2 dashes of Maraschino

juice of ¼ orange

1 tablespoon double cream

Shake well, strain into a medium-sized glass and fill with soda water.

HIGHBALLS

HORSE'S NECK

1½ fl oz brandy

2 dashes of Angostura bitters

2 cubes of ice

Use a long tumbler and fill with ginger ale. Peel the rind of a lemon spirally in one piece and place one end over the edge of the tumbler, allowing the remainder to curl inside.

SPRITZER

½ dry white wine

½ soda water

Build into a large ice-filled glass. Add a twist of lemon.

JULEPS

'One of the most delightful and insinuating potations that ever was invented,' the English novelist Captain Marryat RN wrote in his diary while travelling through the southern United States in 1838. It was he who introduced the beverage to the British Isles.

PINEAPPLE JULEP (for 6 people)

juice of 2 oranges

2 fl oz raspberry vinegar

2 fl oz Maraschino

3 fl oz gin

1 bottle of sparkling Moselle or Saumur

Fill a large glass jug quarter-full with crushed ice. Pour in the ingredients. Pull a pineapple to pieces with a silver fork and place the pieces in the jug. Stir the mixture and decorate with a little fresh fruit.

SOUTHERN MINT JULEP

4 sprigs of fresh mint

1½ teaspoons powdered sugar

2 fl oz bourbon or rye whisky

Use a long tumbler and crush the mint leaves and sugar together lightly. Add the whisky and fill the glass with cracked ice. Stir gently until the glass is frosted. Decorate with 3 sprigs of fresh mint.

RICKEYS

Rickeys can be made with any spirit or liqueur. Put 2 fl oz of the chosen spirit or liqueur, the juice of ½ lime or ¼ lemon and a cube of ice in a medium-sized glass, and top up with carbonated water.

SAVOY RICKEY

1 cube of ice

juice of ½ lime or ¼ lemon

2 fl oz gin

4 dashes of Grenadine

Fill with carbonated water and leave the rind of lime or lemon in the glass.

SLINGS

GIN SLING

1 teaspoon sugar dissolved in water

2 fl oz dry gin

1 cube of ice

Serve in a long tumbler and fill with water or soda water. It can be served hot with a little nutmeg grated on top.

SINGAPORE SLING

juice of ¼ lemon

⅔ dry gin

⅓ cherry brandy

Shake well, strain into a medium-sized glass and fill with soda water. Add a cube of ice.

SOURS

A sour is usually prepared from the following recipe:

juice of ½ lemon

1 teaspoon sugar

2 fl oz spirit or liqueur

Shake well and strain into a medium-sized glass. Add a squirt of soda water and a slice of orange with a maraschino cherry.

EGG SOUR

1 teaspoon powdered white sugar

2 dashes of fresh lemon juice

1 fl oz Curaçao

1 fl oz brandy

1 egg

2–3 small cubes of ice

Shake well and remove the ice before serving.

ACKNOWLEDGEMENTS

Special thanks to Ian Coleman, Giorgio Locatelli, Ian Moore, David Sharland
and Peter Dorelli for their help in the preparation of this book.

INDEX